A GUIDEBOOK TO CONTEMPORARY ARCHITECTURE IN TORONTO

A GUIDEBOOK TO CONTEMPORARY ARCHITECTURE IN TORONTO

MARGARET GOODFELLOW
PHIL GOODFELLOW

INTERVIEWS WITH
BRUCE KUWABARA
LARRY WAYNE RICHARDS
WILLIAM THORSELL

ESSAY BY
SHAWN MICALLEF

SERIES EDITORS
NANCY DUNTON
HELEN MALKIN

DOUGLAS & McINTYRE

Douglas and McIntyre (2013) Ltd.
Box 219, Madeira Park BC
Canada V0N 2H0
www.douglas-mcintyre.com

Library and Archives Canada
Cataloguing in Publication

Goodfellow, Margaret, 1977–
   A guidebook to contemporary architecture in Toronto / Margaret Goodfellow and Phil Goodfellow.

Includes indexes.
ISBN 978-1-55365-444-5

   1. Architecture—Ontario—Toronto—Guidebooks. 2. Toronto (Ont.)—Buildings, structures, etc.—Guidebooks.
I. Goodfellow, Phil, 1977– II. Title.

NA747.T6G65 2010
720.9713'54109051   C2009-905739-5

Printed and bound in China by C & C Offset Printing Co., Ltd.
Printed on acid-free paper
Distributed in the U.S. by Publishers Group West

Texts: Margaret Goodfellow & Phil Goodfellow
Editing: Lynda Muir
Series Editors: Nancy Dunton & Helen Malkin
Cartography: Flavio Trevisan
Research: Scott Keyes

Book Design: George Vaitkunas
Front cover and construction photos: As indicated in credits
Mentor Group: James Chavel, Amy Lin, Michael McClelland, Scott Sørli, Flavio Trevisan

Special Thanks: Matthew Galvin, Bruce Kuwabara, Shawn Micallef, Larry Wayne Richards, William Thorsell, David Steiner, Kathy Vey, Jessica Waese

    The Royal Architectural Institute of Canada L'Institut royal d'architecture du Canada

The authors gratefully acknowledge the financial support of the Toronto Society of Architects and the Royal Architectural Institute of Canada Foundation in the preparation of this book.

Additional thanks go to the authors' families, friends and colleagues for their thoughtful input and endless support.

Dedicated to our grandparents

 Canada Council for the Arts Conseil des Arts du Canada

The publisher gratefully acknowledges the financial support of the Canada Council for the Arts, the British Columbia Arts Council, the Province of British Columbia through the Book Publishing Tax Credit and the Government of Canada through the Book Publishing Industry Development Program (BPIDP) for its publishing activities.

CONTENTS

PREFACE

Why this book?

Over the past fifteen years, Toronto has undergone a dramatic architectural transformation that has reshaped our perception of the city. Public and private investment in Toronto's academic institutions and neighbourhoods, together with the *Cultural Renaissance*, characterized by a significant injection of funding for the city's cultural institutions, have generated an array of new projects in the city. Most important, design excellence has been the key factor in this building boom.

This guidebook documents a critical mass of projects completed between 1992 and 2010. Its portable, accessible format will aid in the navigation to and discovery of contemporary architecture in Toronto.

Why these buildings?

The selected projects reflect contemporary tendencies, aspirations and attitudes toward city building. In developing the selection, we asked ourselves the following questions: Do these projects represent excellence in design? Do they represent our contemporary period? Have they acted as transformational agents? Do they use materials and detailing in an innovative way? Do they propose new models of city building? Finally, and most important, would we insist that our friends visit these places?

Many of the structures chosen represent a reinvestment in the historic building fabric. The reintegration of such buildings into the city is an essential contribution to the city's collective memory, and reminds us of our often under-appreciated history.

For the most part, the selected projects are either publicly accessible or accessible by paid admission. A few of the buildings are private, but they are worth a visit even if only to be seen from the outside. For those selections, we have included drawings and interior photographs intended to illustrate some unique aspects of their design.

While hotel, restaurant and retail interiors often fit the above criteria, they are not included in this book because of their ephemeral nature. There are numerous publications that promote and publish these innovative spaces.

Toronto's particular morphology has produced local residential typologies, including laneway, infill and ravine housing. We have included a few examples when they are located within our defined neighbourhoods, but we acknowledge that there are many that have been left out.

Are there exceptional projects that should have been included but were not? Perhaps, but given the criteria outlined above, the selections reinforce the narrative of our contemporary period, fit within our defined neighbourhoods, and have been built or had major urban components completed by 2010 as prerequisites for inclusion in this volume.

Why this time period?

In the wake of the recession of 1990–91, and the economic stagnation that succeeded it, 1995 marked the beginning of the longest period of sustained economic growth in Toronto since the end of World War II. The quickened pace of development that occurred in these years establishes the guidebook's context and the framework for our selection of contemporary projects.

Although we can point to no singular watershed moment, the transformation of Toronto cannot be discussed without examining two exceptional projects that were harbingers of things to come. In 1992, the opening of the Allen Lambert Galleria at BCE Place (now called Brookfield Place) reintroduced the inspirational qualities of design excellence to Toronto. Santiago Calatrava's exquisite Galleria blended new public space, private investment and architectural delight with a skill that had not been seen since Viljo Revell's Toronto City Hall of 1964. In 1995, the privately funded Bata Shoe Museum opened, foretelling the rise of philanthropic investment in the city's cultural institutions. These two buildings are exemplars of the new cultural and economic models that would become the standard for development.

Nor could we examine the transformation of Toronto without also discussing the global impact of the "Bilbao Effect," a process by which cities were reinventing themselves through high-profile architectural projects. During this period, governments increasingly recognized the positive impact that "the business of culture" has on the economy. Locally, initiatives such as the Ontario SuperBuild Corporation and the Canada-Ontario Infrastructure Program provided base capital funding for academic and cultural institutions, promoting partnerships between the public and private sectors. These institutions then sought out the best Canadian and international architects to raise the profile of their projects and create attractive philanthropic opportunities.

A thriving design community has long existed in Toronto, but the development of a critical mass of high-profile projects from 1992 onward stimulated clients, philanthropists and the public to demand excellence in the design of their city. Not since the buoyant optimism of the 1960s has Toronto experienced the kind of cultural confidence manifested by the selections in this guidebook.

Who was this book written for?

In one word, you. Torontonians and visitors – people who are interested in architecture, landscape architecture and the development of contemporary urban form.

The purpose of this guide is to enable the reader to find buildings and places in Toronto, and to understand each project's context, key attributes and merits.

We encourage you to take this handy guidebook and explore the streets of our vibrant metropolis.

HOW TO USE THIS BOOK

The projects are grouped according to neighbourhood, and their names correspond to those on city maps and signage. Maps of the neighbourhoods are oriented towards nominal Toronto north – to a Torontonian, Yonge Street runs north-south and Bloor Street east-west, with Lake Ontario being south. Streetcar lines, bus routes and subway stations have been indicated on each map, along with walking distances and times. A short text about each neighbourhood gives the visitor a sense of the historical context, its defining qualities and other projects in the area that are of note.

The neighbourhoods are numbered and projects are ordered in an implied sequence to guide the reader to the next neighbourhood, which is typically in close proximity. We have keyed the maps with arrows and page numbers to indicate the adjacent neighbourhoods. Although we have suggested an order, we invite you to explore Toronto in a way that makes sense to you.

The buildings and places in this guidebook are all accessible by the Toronto Transit Commission (TTC). For each project, we have identified TTC options including subways, streetcars and buses. All TTC surface routes connect with the subway system. Streetcar routes are noted by route number and name, though the name on the front of the streetcar will denote its final destination – for example, 501 Queen may appear as 501 Roncesvalles on the streetcar. Please check with the TTC for details on the hours, frequency, and fares (www.ttc.ca).

Every attempt has been made to be clear about the reader's access to the projects. For those buildings that are not open to the public, we ask readers to respect people's right to privacy.

The architects, landscape architects, and urban designers are identified by the name of the firm at the time of project completion. To the best of our knowledge the current name of the firm has also been indicated. Indexes are organized by building, building type and design firm to allow for easy cross-referencing.

Images of the projects are typically, but not exclusively, those that the designers themselves use to present their work, and in most cases show the project as it was at the time of completion. We would like to thank the designers, clients, and photographers alike who responded to our request for drawings and images.

INTERVIEW WITH BRUCE KUWABARA, LARRY WAYNE RICHARDS AND WILLIAM THORSELL

In the research and preparation for this guidebook, we interviewed three people who were key agents in the transformation of Toronto. This transformation is characterized by significant public and private investment in academic, residential, institutional and *Cultural Renaissance* projects. The *Cultural Renaissance* projects include the Royal Ontario Museum, Art Gallery of Ontario, Canadian Opera Company, Royal Conservatory of Music, Canada's National Ballet School, Young Centre for the Performing Arts, renovations to Roy Thomson Hall, and the Gardiner Museum. These three people offer perspectives from their vantage points as architectural practitioner, academic and client. Each was interviewed separately during May and June 2009, and their responses to our questions are compiled below.

Bruce Kuwabara is an architect and design partner at Kuwabara Payne McKenna Blumberg Architects in Toronto. Larry Wayne Richards is a professor and the former Dean of the John H. Daniels Faculty of Architecture, Landscape, and Design at the University of Toronto. William Thorsell is the Director and Chief Executive Officer of the Royal Ontario Museum (ROM).

On the Cultural Renaissance

What are your thoughts on the outcome of the Cultural Renaissance?

Bruce Kuwabara, June 26, 2009: I think the most remarkable thing about the projects of the *Cultural Renaissance* is that they were all completed. What is impressive is that every single one of the clients found a way to get their vision funded and built.

William Thorsell, June 8, 2009: Daniel Libeskind reminded me early on that a lot of great projects never get built. You can win a competition and the project may never see the light of day. When he was at the ROM's public events, he used to always point out that buildings need clients who can actually see them through, work with the architects, and work with communities. The client is often the missing player in people's minds; they see the architect, they see the funders, but there has to be a client who plays a role.

How did government funding support the Cultural Renaissance?

WT: Back in 2002, when the provincial government announced that it was going to fund four projects and wanted the federal government to match their funding, the federal government decided it wanted two additional projects to be funded. So both governments ended up funding six projects together. It was a very interesting moment, and a very fortunate one for Toronto that there was a public program to seed capital projects.

Former Premier Mike Harris weighed in very heavily that the provincial government was going to finance major cultural projects. Some of his caucus wanted to spread the funding all over the place, to every little place. We argued against that and said that they had to be strategic with their funding.

Following Toronto's loss of the 2008 Summer Olympic bid, I went to see Mike Harris and said, "You have a Plan B, which you probably don't even know about. It is all these cultural and institutional applications that are sitting on your desk right now. And if you don't worry too much about favouring Toronto, you can give them a head start, and they could be done quicker than the Olympics, and last a lot longer."

[Premier Harris] saw that, though he doesn't get credit for it because people just see him as someone who ruined the city. But in fact, he did some things wrong, and some things right; and many of the things that he did right came from *SuperBuild*. The Toronto Waterfront Revitalization Corporation formed under his regime. New buildings for universities, colleges and hospitals were also supported by *SuperBuild* funding. He got a lot of leverage out of that capital – it was a very high leverage for public money.

Though this seed government money funded almost 30 percent of the projects, more than 70 percent of the money came from the private sector. You had individuals and companies that could come up with a couple hundred million dollars for the ROM or a couple hundred million for the AGO, and so forth.

Bruce, previously you have discussed the importance of the Cultural Renaissance in relation to its creation of cultural platforms. What is a cultural platform?

BK: The cultural platform is a metaphor. You can take it literally if you want, but it is a metaphor for giving the cultural institutions the right kind of infra-structure that has long-term value and is able to support not only their current programming, but expanded thinking about future programming.

My perspective on the Cultural Renaissance has shifted over the last two years. I have gone from designing the buildings to being one of the participants in the lives of the cultural institutions themselves. I am a frequent visitor to the Gardiner Museum, will attend concerts at the Royal Conservatory of Music, take my daughter to classes at Canada's National Ballet School, and often bring my children to what they refer to as "The Triangle Museum".

Though Toronto-based practitioners have shaped the Cultural Renaissance as much as international practitioners, how has the influx of new architec-tural ideas changed Toronto?

BK: I am very interested in how much the city has been transformed by wave after wave of influence from international sources – either by transplants or architects invited to Toronto for a single project. That was the case with Daniel Libeskind, Frank Gehry, and Will Alsop. Will they ever build here again? Who knows? But they have had a significant effect on our culture, and the quality of architecture in this city.

The history of architecture in Toronto is much more about this tension between what is here and what is coming in from elsewhere. The idea of Toronto as an open heterogeneous system, oscillating between external and local forces of influence is important. Foreign architects – Viljo Revell, Mies van der Rohe, Frank Gehry – may have produced many of our most significant buildings. However, in terms of the ongoing transformation of the city, local decision-makers, developers, architects, landscape architects, and designers have a more pervasive impact on the overall quality of urban life, and therefore, must assume responsibility for how Toronto works as a sustainable city in which design really matters.

On the Renaissance ROM

Was an international architectural competition always seen as the key vehicle for the museum's redevelopment?

WT: Yes, right off the bat. We wanted to do the competition for a number of reasons. One, we wanted to see who was out there, what they would do. And two, the Guggenheim Museum in Bilbao drew our attention to a new form of architecture, which was leaving the International Style behind. It just so happened that as we were saying that we needed to break out of the consensus that is Toronto, and that we needed to break out of the state that the museum was in, we ran into this moment in architectural history when there were suddenly a number of very credible and interesting architects who were no longer bound by ideology. They could express themselves using a program; they could express themselves personally; they could bring in poetic aspects to buildings that were there for reasons that had nothing to do with efficiency or form. They have to do with function, and in a broader sense of what function really is. It is partly the function of major buildings like the ROM to be a symbol, and to speak about other things than efficiencies.

As soon as we announced that we were having an architectural competition, there was a huge amount of coverage right away. At last, we were going to see what was going to happen. There was no public competition for any of the other *Cultural Renaissance* projects. We are the ones that went out and said, "We don't know who the architect is going to be, and let's all come in and have a big discussion about it." And I think that was one of the great virtues of the *Renaissance ROM* project.

How important was the architectural competition to raising the ROM's profile?

WT: The competition was a critical part of our fundraising strategy. It was part of this building up of a sense that the city needed something marvelous, wonderful and risky, so that it could be funded. That is why we started with seven architects and an exhibition that showed all of their models. And then we had public forums when we got down to three architects; we had another exhibition along with the architects making public presentations at the ROM. On the first night, Andrea Bruno presented and six hundred people came. On the second night, Bing Thom presented and another six hundred people came. Finally, Daniel Libeskind presented his scheme and sixteen hundred people came out on a February night to listen to an architect say what he wanted to do with a corner of the city.

During that presentation, we noted Libeskind's skills, his ability to inspire and his ability to generate a sense of excitement, which helped build support behind the project. Libeskind was very helpful to us from the point of view of momentum and attracting support.

There was a tremendous amount of public interest as a result of the competition, which got the government's attention. This was very interesting because at the end of the competition, when we said we would be announcing our finalist the next day, the provincial Minister of Culture called and asked, "Do you think I could make the announcement of your choice?" I said, "Absolutely." It was then that I knew we would get the financial support from the government and enthusiasm from the public.

On reinvesting in the University of Toronto

What were some of the driving forces behind the University's expansion?

Larry Wayne Richards, May 22, 2009: In the mid to late 1990s, the University, under President Robert Prichard, decided that they wanted to guarantee accommodation for first year students. The University was becoming aware of this need because the cost of rental units in Toronto was going up, and enrolment was growing. The University of Toronto is always struggling with its image and reality as a commuter university. The two suburban campuses, though they have built more residences, are essentially commuter places. The St. George campus, which has in excess of 45,000 students, has approximately 6,000 student resident spaces.

The University decided that it wanted to build more student residence spaces, creating a stronger sense of community on the St. George campus. It assembled a secondary plan, which identified development sites on the St. George campus. These development sites identified the extent of construction allowable governed by the urban design guidelines particular to each site. It was a landmark agreement between the University and the City, and is now a by-law.

The first project of the new student housing initiative was Graduate House. The second one was New College Residence; the third was Woodsworth College Residence. And then finally, University College built its infill residence tower. Another project that I really regret didn't happen was the Student Residence at Varsity Stadium. Though there were various starts and stops for the site, the best scheme that I saw over the years was the Baird Sampson Neuert Architects' project that integrated the athletic facilities with housing. I would say that it was the last bold study from the Robert Prichard era, but unfortunately, that particular Varsity project did not happen. Ultimately, the initiative to provide a lot more student housing was a success because it got four major residential projects built; then it sort of faded out.

More importantly, a high-level committee had been struck at the University to address the need for better design. Woodsworth College by Kuwabara

Payne McKenna Blumberg Architects (with Barton Myers Associates) had been completed, and everybody said, "Wow, we can do something really good!" Woodsworth College, completed in 1992, set a new standard in terms of design for the University. This led to the new Design Review Committee with the mandate to set the design bar very high.

When the proposal to build Graduate House popped up, we pushed quickly for a competition. Janice Oliver, who was assistant vice-president of Operations and Services at the University, was very skilled politically and close to Rob Prichard. There was an openness and willingness to do things. He recognized the value of good architecture and how excellence can be achieved through quality facilities and civic spaces. As the new dean of the Faculty of Architecture, Landscape and Design in 1997, I pushed very hard and very fast for design excellence.

My argument for an architectural competition was, "If the University of Toronto claims to be an international university, why aren't the searches for the designers of major buildings international?" There were many good arguments against it: everything from costs, inefficiencies, and the question of strong local talent versus international talent. Nevertheless, we set up this limited invitational competition and there were five schemes. Stephen Teeple teamed up with Morphosis from Los Angeles and won the project.

What was the community's response to the project?

LWR: Graduate House was very controversial because of its aggressive relationship to the public realm. It brought people from all sides into a public forum discussing architecture. Some members of the public decried everything – from the style and look of the building to the fact that parts of the building hung into public space.

It was also a very difficult process because the contractor went bankrupt during construction, and the building sat for months with nothing happening. But it finally got built on an incredibly low budget. Thom Mayne of Morphosis would always joke, "You know the only thing I've been able to build on that kind of budget before was a parking garage." He couldn't believe how low the budget was, and people overlook that sometimes.

So it got built generating a lot of successes, some weaknesses, and some valid questions including what it means to be contextual in the neighborhood. Graduate House caused the surrounding community to become much more active and organized.

On reinterpreting Toronto's past

What has Toronto's approach been to preserving and managing its built heritage?

LWR: Every great city that I admire has a strong heritage component, both in terms of preserving and managing its built heritage. From the federal government on down the line to the municipality, the recognition of the value of heritage is still quite weak in Canada and Toronto, and I get very upset about it. In my nine years on the Board of the Ontario Heritage Trust, I was a bit of a thorn in the side of Queen's Park. Colleagues and I at the Trust had more than one meeting with the Minister of Culture arguing for stronger initiatives to protect heritage through various incentives. There isn't enough support like low or no-interest loans, or substantial grants for individuals who have a house with heritage value. Developers need stronger incentives too. In terms of heritage preservation, too much is still being torn down.

What was Libeskind's approach to built heritage at the ROM?

WT: There are some very good modernist architects in Toronto who know how to do respectful juxtapositions of modern and heritage structures. Libeskind's approach is a much more radical juxtaposition. The Crystal is not meant to take a cue from something, it is meant to be an equal conversation between two buildings and two ideas. It is saying, "We both have great ideas and we are going to go like this." It is an interesting thing; the city is big and it needs both types of building to happen.

How has the design of the Crystal put into focus aspects of the ROM that may have previously been obscured?

WT: The historical façades, which one never used to notice because they were in the background, suddenly now have become star objects on the inside of the heritage wings. You can now appreciate the former exterior elevation of the two wings, because of the radical juxtaposition of the Crystal. While we were going through construction, Daniel Libeskind pointed out how the two buildings related to each other. I said to him, "You know, it is like a relationship where you knew Tom and you knew Mary, but if they get married, there is a new thing called Tom and Mary, who have a new identity." There is a third identity called their relationship. And what we saw happening as the Crystal took its shape and form was this third identity emerging. The spaces, volumes and textures emerged almost like a surprise, although they were always there.

On Toronto's next project

Following this Cultural Renaissance, what is the next great project for Toronto?

BK: The next great project is sustainable urbanism at the larger scale. The leading edge of sustainability is moving towards a more low-tech, local and socially driven agenda. I believe we need to focus on creative, integrative thinking in a way that brings together sustainability, urbanism, architecture, landscape and design. We need to think about sustaining the public realm and nurturing neighbourhoods as the most important acts of city-building. This is also a time for us to think, assess and evaluate what has been going on. There have been shifts in the right direction. Regent Park is a good shift. The waterfront is a complete shift from what was there before. The WaveDecks are important, because they are threading back and reconnecting the part of the waterfront that I think of as sort of the badlands. I mean, it is tough down there.

WT: I think that the big job for the city is the public interstitial space – all of the connective tissue, which is still in a dreadful state of disrepair and lacking imagination and care. It is the public living room spaces that tie it all together, that connect everything, but that are just falling apart, right, left and centre. We are not organized to deal with public space in a coherent fashion in this city. It is a good project for the next municipal administration to say, "Let's get back down to where we actually live." There is an opportunity for people to come forward and start talking about a city that is beautiful in the public space, not just in the institutional or the private buildings.

LWR: The lack of resolution around mobility issues in Toronto will come home to roost very soon. Toronto has done little to discourage the use of the private automobile in the inner city, which is generating more and more traffic congestion. This has generated a kind of warfare between drivers, cyclists, and pedestrians. It's not efficient, increasingly dangerous, and not very civilized. So I think the next big project requires a confrontation with the current mobility mess and the creation of an exciting, workable vision of how people, vehicles, public transport, and goods can move efficiently, safely, and gracefully throughout an expanding, dense Toronto.

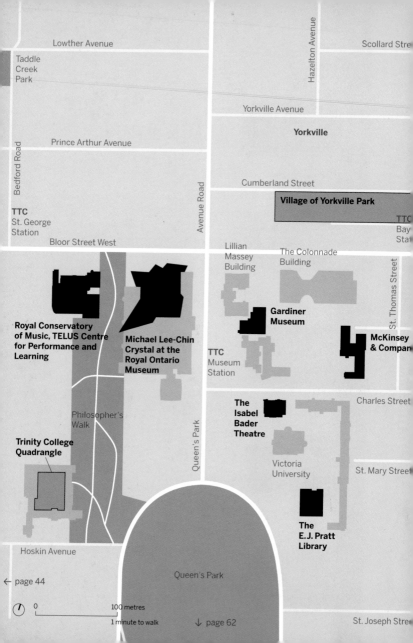

Lowther Avenue

Taddle
Creek
Park

Hazelton Avenue

Scollard Stre

Prince Arthur Avenue

Yorkville Avenue

Yorkville

Bedford Road

Avenue Road

Cumberland Street

Village of Yorkville Park

TTC
Bay
Sta

TTC
St. George
Station

Bloor Street West

Lillian
Massey
Building

The Colonnade
Building

St. Thomas Street

**Royal Conservatory
of Music, TELUS Centre
for Performance and
Learning**

**Michael Lee-Chin
Crystal at the
Royal Ontario
Museum**

**Gardiner
Museum**

**McKinsey
& Compan**

TTC
Museum
Station

Philosopher's
Walk

Queen's Park

Charles Street

**The
Isabel
Bader
Theatre**

**Trinity College
Quadrangle**

Victoria
University

St. Mary Street

**The
E. J. Pratt
Library**

Hoskin Avenue

← page 44

0   100 metres

1 minute to walk

Queen's Park

↓ page 62

St. Joseph Stre

BLOOR / YORKVILLE

The former Village of Yorkville was annexed by the City of Toronto in 1883. The quiet, residential character of this neighbourhood was transformed in the 1960s when it became the centre of Toronto's counter-culture movement. Subsequent increases in land value led to the high-end commercial and retail development that is characteristic of Yorkville today.

Skirting along the southern edge of Yorkville, Bloor Street West is a shopping destination, home to the city's most exclusive retail establishments. The Bloor Street Transformation, a streetscaping initiative, will elevate the quality of the public realm to match the calibre of its retail tenants and patrons. The address for many of the city's prominent cultural institutions, Bloor Street also marks the northern edge of the St. George campus of the University of Toronto.

Unlike the adjacent bustling commercial district, Victoria University, a federated university within the University of Toronto, is a pedestrian-friendly green refuge. A distinct campus within of the University of Toronto, it was established on the eastern edge of Queen's Park in 1892. The area is characterized by a series of stately ivy-covered academic buildings and quadrangles.

VILLAGE OF YORKVILLE PARK

Built over an existing subway line, this compact park is an example of Toronto's commitment to urbanize nature and naturalize the city. The winning scheme from a 1991 design competition generated controversy because of its overtly artificial representation of nature. The park's success is to due to the vision of then Parks and Recreation commissioner Herb Pirk and the Bloor-Yorkville Business Improvement Area association, who helped transform this former parking lot into a favourite urban retreat.

Disparate landscapes come together in the design of this park. Described as a series of Victorian curiosity boxes, ten discrete gardens each represent a different type of natural Canadian landscape. These groupings are based on forest, meadow, marsh, prairie and the Canadian Shield, creating a variety of sensory experiences connected through pedestrian paths and paving patterns. The 650-ton granite mound was controversial when first proposed, but is now a much-admired element in the life of the park.

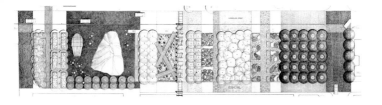

Landscape Architect **Schwartz/Smith/Meyer Landscape Architects Ltd.**
Architect **Oleson Worland Architects**
Client **City of Toronto**
Completed **1994**
Address **Cumberland Street at Bellair Street**
Subway **Yonge-University-Spadina Line, Bay Station**
Access **public**

GARDINER MUSEUM

Although the Gardiner Museum has been open at its current location since 1984, the recent expansion to house its renowned ceramics collection is a critical project in Toronto's Cultural Renaissance.

The museum is set behind a landscaped forecourt and respects the classical façade of the Lillian Massey building. Sheathed in stone and glass, the structure features a projecting volume of Indiana limestone, which announces and shelters the main entrance while creating a rooftop terrace.

The lobby, with its long reception desk elegantly finished in white oak, draws visitors deep into the building. The interior renovation is focused on three new gallery spaces, expanded educational facilities, and a ground-floor gift shop. Top-lit stairs lead to the third-floor Terrace Room, where the Royal Ontario Museum's historic façade provides a backdrop for diners and patrons alike.

Architect	**Kuwabara Payne McKenna Blumberg Architects**
Landscape Architect	**NAK Design**
Client	**Gardiner Museum**
Completed	**2006**
Address	**111 Queen's Park**
Subway	**Yonge-University-Spadina Line, Museum Station**
Access	**paid admission, www.gardinermuseum.com**

McKINSEY & COMPANY

The Canadian headquarters for McKinsey & Company is a commercial office building that reinforces the academic nature of its surroundings. On the boundary between Yorkville and Victoria University, this facility is the result of an unconventional arrangement that will see the building turned over to the university for academic use at the end of its lease.

The building is situated to maintain pedestrian connections, frame views and reinforce the courtyard typology of the campus. The building's massing is characterized by the low-slung south pavilion, which addresses the domestic scale of Charles Street while concealing the tall, deep mass along Sultan Street. A private courtyard, defined by a low garden wall, opens onto the adjacent green space.

The exterior is handsomely finished in rough and smooth-cut Owen Sound limestone, which references both the rough stone of the university and the smooth concrete of the Colonnade building to the north. The windows are framed in rich teak and mahogany, with mullions that add colour and rhythm to the façade. An interior, curving, three-storey atrium, inaccessible to the public, belies the orthogonal nature of the exterior.

Architect	**Taylor Hariri Pontarini Architects**
Landscape Architect	**The MBTW Group**
Client	**McKinsey & Company, Victoria University**
Completed	**1999**
Address	**10 Charles Street West**
Subway	**Yonge-University-Spadina Line, Museum Station**
Access	**private**

THE ISABEL BADER THEATRE

This small theatre responds elegantly to the built context of Charles Street, encloses a quadrangle, and strengthens connections through Victoria University. Together with the McKinsey & Company building across the street, the theatre establishes a contemporary language with traditional, contextual materials.

The tall, vertical rhythm of the north elevation and the use of stone acknowledge the Gothic traditions of the university. A thick carpet of green ivy links the blank south façade of the auditorium with the neighbouring Neo-Gothic Burwash Hall.

The stone and wood-lined lobby frames views towards the Richardsonian Romanesque Victoria University building. The 500-seat auditorium has a high degree of flexibility and can function as a lecture hall or live performance venue for the university, and the community.

Architect **Lett/Smith Architects**
Client **Victoria University**
Completed **2001**
Address **93 Charles Street West**
Subway **Yonge-University-Spadina Line, Museum Station**
Access **university hours, www.utoronto.ca**

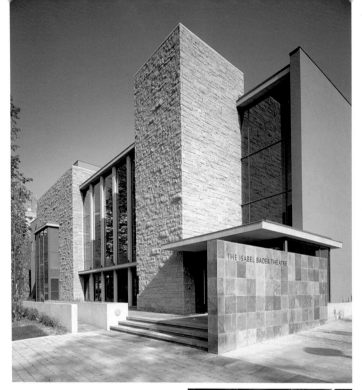

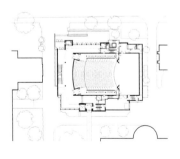

THE E. J. PRATT LIBRARY

Named in honour of a renowned poet and academic, this modernist box, originally designed by Gordon S. Adamson and Associates in 1960, required extensive renovations to meet the needs of today's students. Though the Credit Valley sandstone exterior was left untouched, strategic interior interventions refreshed this well-loved library with a colourful graphic sensibility.

The main space is a vast double-height reading room under a playful ceiling of round acoustic tiles. The mezzanine level provides a variety of intimate and communal study spaces. Veiled by a fritted glass screen, a bright red wall anchors the central staircase, where daylight is drawn from two circular skylights. On the lower level, a student lounge and study carrels overlook the intimate Lester B. Pearson Garden for Peace and Understanding, designed by landscape architect Paul Ehnes.

Architect **Kohn Shnier Architects / Shore Tilbe Irwin & Partners**
Client **Victoria University**
Completed **2001**
Address **71 Queen's Park Crescent**
Subway **Yonge-University-Spadina Line, Museum Station**
Access **university hours, www.utoronto.ca**

TRINITY COLLEGE QUADRANGLE

The Trinity College Quadrangle is a hidden gem at the University of Toronto. The result of a design competition, the quad is a complete reimagining of what was once a less-than-extraordinary courtyard cluttered with benches and garbage cans. The new landscape reflects the tradition of medieval courtyards and the spiritual aspirations of the college.

Trinity College was founded in 1851 by John Strachan, the first Anglican Bishop of Toronto. Originally located within what is now Trinity Bellwoods Park on Queen Street West, Trinity College moved to the University of Toronto St. George campus in 1925. The root of the stylized *X* pattern is inspired by the Greek letter *chi*, which was adopted as a symbol for Christ by early Christians. Only existing trees interrupt the rigorous patterning of this symbol in tracery form.

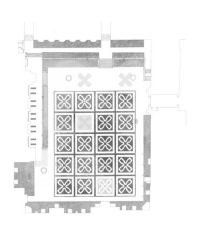

Architect & Landscape Architect **gh3**

Client **University of Toronto**

Completed **2007**

Address **6 Hoskin Avenue**

Subway **Yonge-University-Spadina Line, Museum Station**

Access **weekdays only, www.utoronto.ca**

MICHAEL LEE-CHIN CRYSTAL AT THE ROYAL ONTARIO MUSEUM

The international architectural competition for the Renaissance ROM redevelopment project sparked an unprecedented fundraising campaign and a lively public discussion on architecture in Toronto. Daniel Libeskind's winning proposal was conceived on a cocktail napkin and inspired by the ROM's minerals and gems collection.

After the demolition of a 1980s era addition, Torontonians watched in awe as over 3,000 steel members were dynamically assembled to form the Michael Lee-Chin Crystal. While it was originally envisioned as a glazed crystal, programmatic requirements necessitated a greater opacity. The structure is clad in a skin of warm silver aluminum strips, and controlled daylight permeates via a series of composed slashes.

The Crystal fuses the wings of the existing museum to create a "mixing chamber" that showcases and reinterprets the ROM's many assets. The spectacular dinosaur collection is displayed in a gallery-like space, hovering in a shard above Bloor Street West. In the Hyacinth Chen Crystal Court, stalactite-shaped lightwells illuminate the buff brick corbels and arched windows of the heritage building. The redevelopment also restores clarity to the original building by making a formal entrance on Bloor Street West and opening axial views to Philosopher's Walk. Atop the Crystal, the C5 restaurant features stunning vistas across a landscaped green roof to the city beyond.

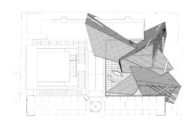

Architect	**Studio Daniel Libeskind / B+H Architects**
Landscape Architect	**Quinn Design Associates**
Rooftop Garden	**PLANT Architects**
Heritage Architect	**ERA Architects**
Client	**Royal Ontario Museum**
Completed	**2007**
Address	**100 Queen's Park**
Subway	**Yonge-University-Spadina Line, Museum Station**
Access	**paid admission, www.rom.on.ca**

ROYAL CONSERVATORY OF MUSIC, TELUS CENTRE FOR PERFORMANCE AND LEARNING

The restoration, renovation and expansion of the Royal Conservatory of Music's home has been more than ten years in the making. Brought about by public, corporate and private funding, a restored McMaster Hall now plays a central role in a thoughtful, urbane scheme.

The 1991 Master Plan sought to create a series of great music rooms for both performance and education, in a seamless integration of contemporary and heritage spaces. This intent has been translated into new concert halls, practice rooms and social spaces that respect the proportion, scale and materials of the original building.

The new Siemens Hall is a contemporary interpretation of the original heritage structure with its rough stone exterior and wood framed windows. Along Philosopher's Walk, student rehearsals can be heard from practice rooms below the glazed lobby of the Koerner Concert Hall. The interior of this horseshoe-shaped hall features a veil of twisting wood ribbons that swim across the ceiling before cascading down behind the stage.

Architect	**Kuwabara Payne McKenna Blumberg Architects**
Landscape Architect	**Janet Rosenberg + Associates**
Heritage Architect	**Goldsmith Borgal & Company Ltd. Architects**
Client	**The Royal Conservatory of Music**
Completed	**2009**
Address	**273 Bloor Street West**
Subway	**Yonge-University-Spadina Line, St. George Station**
Access	**public, lobby and atrium only, www.rcmusic.ca**

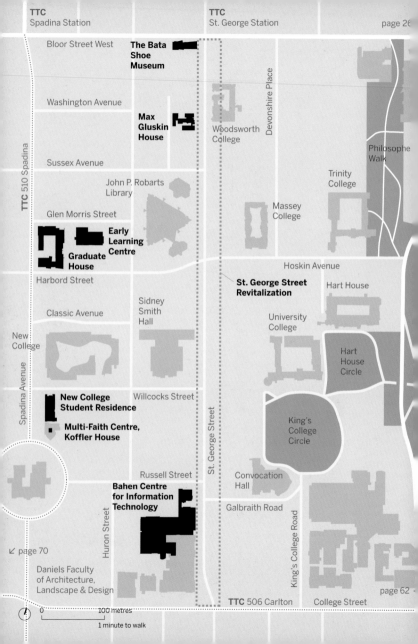

Bloor Street West

The Bata Shoe Museum

Washington Avenue

Max Gluskin House

Devonshire Place

Woodsworth College

Philosophe Walk

Sussex Avenue

TTC 510 Spadina

John P. Robarts Library

Trinity College

Glen Morris Street

Massey College

Early Learning Centre

Graduate House

Harbord Street

Hoskin Avenue

St. George Street Revitalization

Hart House

Classic Avenue

Sidney Smith Hall

University College

New College

Spadina Avenue

Hart House Circle

King's College Circle

New College Student Residence

Willcocks Street

Multi-Faith Centre, Koffler House

Russell Street

St. George Street

Convocation Hall

↙ page 70

Bahen Centre for Information Technology

Galbraith Road

Huron Street

King's College Road

Daniels Faculty of Architecture, Landscape & Design

page 62

TTC 506 Carlton   College Street

0   100 metres
1 minute to walk

UNIVERSITY OF TORONTO – ST. GEORGE CAMPUS

Unlike traditionally introverted university campuses, this downtown home of the University of Toronto is fully integrated into the fabric of the city. Indeed, the city has grown up around the university, blurring the edges between town and gown. Today, the impressive real estate holdings of the St. George campus include over 160 acres of land in the heart of Canada's largest city.

Established in 1827 under a royal charter granted to John Strachan, one of Toronto's formative clerics and intellectuals, the campus has expanded from one of the earliest and most magnificent structures, University College, to include admired buildings such as Hart House and Massey College, and storied open spaces such as Philosopher's Walk and King's College Circle.

In recent years, the university's progressive policies have required design excellence on their three campuses. In 1997, the university established a Design Review Committee, which was armed with the mandate to review the design quality of new capital projects. Together with the University of Toronto Master Plan, these initiatives have led to a wealth of high-calibre buildings and a recognition of the importance of the open space network on its three campuses.

THE BATA SHOE MUSEUM

The Bata Shoe Museum is a sculptural box designed to hold a private collection of over 12,500 shoe-related artifacts. Conceived by Sonja Bata, the wife of shoe magnate Thomas J. Bata, the museum foundation planned for more than fifteen years and reviewed multiple sites before beginning construction on the corner of Bloor Street West and St. George Street. The museum was entirely paid for with private funds, and its operating costs are covered by an endowment fund from the museum foundation.

The angled limestone walls fold back from the street to create a generous pedestrian space, while a bold copper cornice defines the edges of the compact site. A low, broad vitrine cut into the limestone mass hints at the curiosities within. Projecting from a crease in the folding planes, a glazed enclosure leads to the interior. In marked contrast to the solidity of the front façade, the lobby is a sun-drenched volume enlivened by the reflections and shadows cast by the 40-foot-tall art glass installation by Lutz Haufschild.

Architect	**Moriyama & Teshima Architects**
Art Glass	**Lutz Haufschild**
Client	**The Bata Shoe Museum Foundation**
Completed	**1995**
Address	**327 Bloor Street West**
Subway	**Bloor-Danforth Line, St. George Station**
Access	**paid admission, www.batashoemuseum.ca**

UNIVERSITY OF TORONTO – ST. GEORGE CAMPUS

ST. GEORGE STREET REVITALIZATION

The St. George Street Revitalization project set out to repair transportation planning missteps that occurred when the street, which runs through the heart of the campus, was widened to accommodate increased vehicular traffic. The outcome of an urban design competition, the winning scheme restored the public realm and stitched together a formerly bisected campus.

By a reallocation of space within the street width, room was found for bike lanes, generous sidewalks and trees. Narrower traffic lanes, upgraded paving materials and frequent crosswalks calmed traffic and restored the balance of power among pedestrians, cyclists and automobiles.

Generous planted verges are framed by sculptural concrete elements that buffer pedestrians from the street and serve as benches. The surface of the roadway varies in acknowledgement of the numerous pathways that cross St. George Street. At the centre of the scheme, a new urban square leads to Sidney Smith Hall. The success of this revitalization project led the way for a campus-wide Open Space Master Plan.

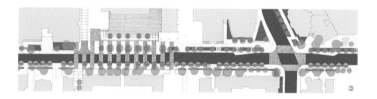

Architect	**Brown + Storey Architects / van Nostrand Di Castri Architects**
Landscape Architect	**Corban and Goode Landscape Architects**
Civil	**City of Toronto Public Works**
Client	**University of Toronto and City of Toronto**
Completed	**1998**
Address	**Between Bloor Street West and College Street**
Subway	**Bloor-Danforth Line, St. George Station**
Streetcar	**506 Carlton**
Access	**public**

MAX GLUSKIN HOUSE, DEPARTMENT OF ECONOMICS

The renovation and expansion of the Department of Economics juxtaposes a crisp contemporary addition with the existing heritage properties. The interior is seamlessly integrated in a warm palette of reclaimed wood. The project was supported by a leading donation from Ira and Maxine Granovsky-Gluskin, who named the building in honour of Ira's father, Max.

The scheme frames two exterior courtyards created by the new additions, clad in a taut skin of ochre-coloured weathering steel and curtain wall. On the interior, heavy timber construction defines the main circulation spaces, while the fine detailing of the wood window surrounds and ceilings provides a sophisticated finish for this academic setting.

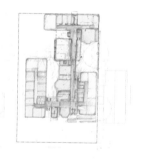

Architect	**Hariri Pontarini Architects**
Landscape Architect	**Janet Rosenberg + Associates**
Heritage Architect	**ERA Architects**
Client	**University of Toronto**
Completed	**2008**
Address	**150 St. George Street**
Subway	**Bloor-Danforth Line, St. George Station**
Access	**university hours, www.utoronto.ca**

UNIVERSITY OF TORONTO – ST. GEORGE CAMPUS

EARLY LEARNING CENTRE

Located in a residential neighbourhood within the university campus, the Early Learning Centre was envisioned as a landscape of play for children. The scale of this building is domestic, but its materiality alludes to its institutional context. A low-slung brick wall supports a rooftop play area, surrounded by a series of shifting Galvalume and glass volumes.

The daycare spaces are organized around a long day-lit ramp, which is revealed on the exterior as it projects from the east elevation. Large play-rooms are scaled for children, with low windows and nooks. Brightly painted lightwells draw daylight inside and provide glimpses to the out-of-doors.

 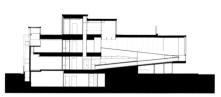

Architect	**Teeple Architects**
Landscape Architect	**The MBTW Group**
Client	**University of Toronto**
Completed	**2003**
Address	**7 Glen Morris Street**
Subway	**Bloor-Danforth Line, Spadina Station**
Streetcar	**510 Spadina**
Access	**lobby only, www.utoronto.ca**

GRADUATE HOUSE

Arguably, of all the selections in this guidebook, no project elicited more controversy in the community and brought more attention to contemporary architecture in Toronto than Graduate House. Born of the University's need to significantly expand student residence space, the building is the result of an international, invited design competition won by Los Angeles based Morphosis and Toronto based Teeple Architects.

Situated at the western edge of the campus, the building is a seven- to ten-storey perimeter block massed around a sunken courtyard. It houses students in two-storey suites, accessed on every other floor. This skip-stop arrangement creates through-units, allowing exposure to air and daylight from both sides.

Bands of charcoal-coloured precast panels clad the Spadina Avenue façade. A contrasting perforated steel screen lightly wraps the curtain wall of the east façade. The entrance is marked by the delamination of the perforated skin, as it slides past the skewed southern block. Dramatically heralding the western gateway to the campus, a cantilevered catwalk emblazoned with the university's name in fritted glass projects over Harbord Street and terminates in the iconic steel O.

Architect	**Morphosis, Teeple Architects**
Landscape Architect	**Janet Rosenberg + Associates**
Client	**University of Toronto**
Completed	**2000**
Address	**60 Harbord Street**
Subway	**Bloor-Danforth Line, Spadina Station**
Streetcar	**510 Spadina**
Access	**lobby only, www.utoronto.ca**

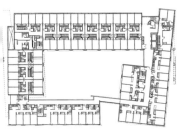

NEW COLLEGE STUDENT RESIDENCE

This residence for New College attempts to balance the contextual needs of the adjacent residential community with the aspirations of a modern university. Built in response to the ongoing need for residence space on campus, it avoided the controversy caused by Graduate House's unapologetic deconstructivist exterior through a thoughtful composition of contextual materials.

A central service spine unites two bar-shaped buildings with distinct identities. While the brick cladding and punched windows of the western bar address the residential character of Spadina Avenue, the strip windows and zinc cladding of the eastern bar address the university's institutional character. A dramatic stairway slices through the central spine that links two large voids containing exterior gardens and amenity spaces.

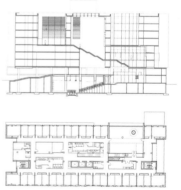

Architect	**Saucier + Perrotte Architectes**
Client	**University of Toronto**
Completed	**2003**
Address	**45 Willcocks Street**
Streetcar	**510 Spadina**
Access	**lobby only, www.utoronto.ca**

MULTI-FAITH CENTRE FOR SPIRITUAL STUDY AND PRACTICE IN THE KOFFLER HOUSE

The Multi-Faith Centre is a skilful insertion of a spiritual, contemplative space into the fabric of a secular university. The design takes on the challenge of creating a meaningful multi-faith setting that speaks to the religious plurality found in Toronto's diverse communities. At its essence, the project explores the transcendental quality of light common to all religions.

The centre is planned as a sequence of venues for the practice and discussion of faith. The main activity hall focuses on a glowing ochre-veined, white onyx feature that wraps the main wall and ceiling. The patterning of this luminous element was developed through an examination of sacred numerology and geometries common among all faiths. The strength of this centre is that its architectural design negotiates the intersection of spirituality and university life in a subtle, welcoming manner.

Architect **Moriyama & Teshima Architects**
Client **University of Toronto**
Completed **2007**
Address **569 Spadina Avenue**
Streetcar **510 Spadina**
Access **university hours, www.utoronto.ca**

BAHEN CENTRE FOR INFORMATION TECHNOLOGY

The Bahen Centre for Information Technology brings together students from the Faculty of Engineering and the Faculty of Arts and Sciences in an academic milieu focused on technological innovation. This infill project creates opportunities out of a neglected site wedged mid-block and bordering on seven existing buildings. Funded and constructed on a fast-track schedule to meet the university's growing enrolment, it was supported by Ontario's SuperBuild Corporation and key donations from John and Margaret Bahen and the founding president of eBay, Jeffrey Skoll.

Clarity within these challenging parameters was achieved through a simple hierarchy of spaces and circulation. The east-west axis features a three-storey arcade incorporating the north façade of the Koffler Centre, while the north-south axis leads to an exterior courtyard. At the intersection of these axes, a monumental stair encircles glazed meeting rooms. From its source in an exterior courtyard defined by the Bahen Centre and its neighbours, a channel of water cascades along a path and connects the building to College Street.

Architect **Diamond + Schmitt Architects**
Landscape Architect **Diamond + Schmitt Architects / Ian Grey & Associates**
Client **University of Toronto**
Completed **2002**
Address **40 St. George Street**
Streetcar **506 Carlton**
Access **university hours, www.utoronto.ca**

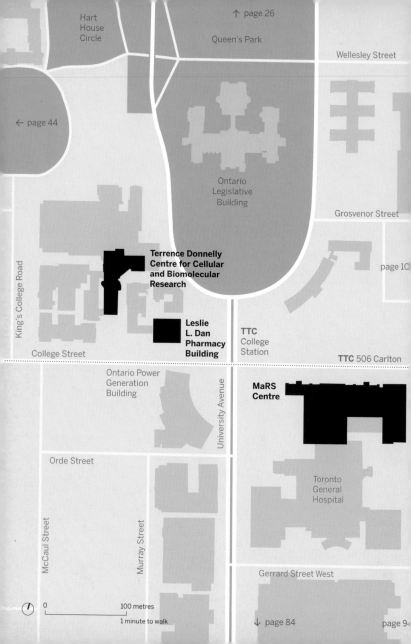

↑ page 26

Hart House Circle

Queen's Park

Wellesley Street

← page 44

Ontario Legislative Building

Grosvenor Street

page 10

King's College Road

Terrence Donnelly Centre for Cellular and Biomolecular Research

Leslie L. Dan Pharmacy Building

TTC College Station

College Street

TTC 506 Carlton

Ontario Power Generation Building

University Avenue

MaRS Centre

Orde Street

Toronto General Hospital

McCaul Street

Murray Street

Gerrard Street West

0   100 metres
1 minute to walk

↓ page 84

page 94

THE DISCOVERY DISTRICT

The Discovery District is the name given to a newly branded precinct encompassing one of the largest concentrations of hospitals, medical research and academic facilities in North America.

University Avenue is Toronto's grand boulevard, designed by landscape architects Dunington-Grubb & Stensson in the 1950s. Lined with hospitals, consulates and financial institutions, University Avenue's centre median is lushly planted and dotted with fountains and sculptures. On the former site of the first building belonging to the University of Toronto, the Ontario Legislative Building now terminates the vista with its asymmetrical Richardsonian Romanesque mass. Designed by Richard Waite and completed in 1893, the pink Credit River valley sandstone exterior is carved with gargoyles, grotesques and friezes.

TERRENCE DONNELLY CENTRE FOR CELLULAR AND BIOMOLECULAR RESEARCH

The result of an international architectural competition, the Terrence Donnelly Centre for Cellular and Biomolecular Research occupies a long and narrow site, made available when Taddle Creek Road was closed. Named after its key donor, this early leader in sustainable design utilizes a double skin on its south façade to minimize heat gain and encourage passive ventilation.

Two six-storey volumes are stacked and set back from College Street, creating a folded, landscaped forecourt. On the interior, this landscape becomes a white terrazzo floor that negotiates the change in grade between the street entrance and the Medical Sciences building to the north. The brick façade of the heritage Rosebrugh building provides a warm backdrop for the terraced garden that runs through the five-storey atrium. Clipped within the atrium are a series of stairs that connect the loft-like research labs. Landscaped lounge spaces distributed throughout allow for informal interaction between researchers.

Architect	**Behnisch Architekten / architectsAlliance**
Landscape Architect	**Diana Gerrard Landscape Architecture**
Client	**University of Toronto**
Completed	**2006**
Address	**160 College Street**
Subway	**Yonge-University-Spadina Line, Queen's Park Station**
Streetcar	**506 Carlton**
Access	**university hours, www.utoronto.ca**

LESLIE L. DAN PHARMACY BUILDING

Sited at the edges of the University of Toronto and the Discovery District, the Leslie L. Dan Pharmacy Building carves out an atypical academic space for students. The twelve-storey building was the winner of an international design competition that drew over twenty submissions. The successful financing of this project was due to funding from Ontario's SuperBuild program, the University Infrastructure Investment Fund and philanthropists, led by a key donation from alumnus and founder of Novopharm, Leslie L. Dan.

A unique corner condition is created when the bulk of the building is lifted to reveal a five-storey atrium framed by slender concrete columns. Suspended in the atrium are two "egg-like" pods that enclose a lecture theatre and a classroom. The tops of these silvery pods create an unusual, inviting study space. At night, the pods become multicoloured orbs, heightening the visual tension between the atrium and the seven-storey building above.

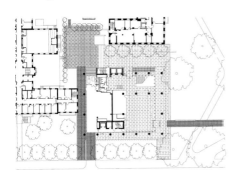

Architect	**Moffat Kinoshita Architects (now Cannon Design)**
Design Consultant	**Foster + Partners**
Lighting Designer	**Claude R. Engle & Lighting Design Solutions/HH Angu**
Client	**University of Toronto**
Completed	**2006**
Address	**144 College Street**
Subway	**Yonge-University-Spadina Line, Queen's Park Station**
Streetcar	**506 Carlton**
Access	**university hours, www.utoronto.ca**

MaRS CENTRE

The MaRS Centre (Medical and Related Sciences) is a non-profit research incubator designed specifically to turn promising academic research into successful commercial products. A multi-million dollar investment by the federal, provincial and municipal governments created a physical hub for knowledge-based research driven by nearby hospitals and universities.

Stretching from University Avenue to Elizabeth Street, the centre is an exemplar of the adaptive reuse that is characteristic of Toronto. The College Wing, formerly home to the Toronto General Hospital, will knit together the Phase 1 Medical Discovery Tower and the planned Phase 2 tower. Through the preservation of the College Wing, the design maintains its landscaped forecourt, a welcoming respite along busy College Street.

The fifteen-storey Medical Discovery Tower houses adaptable medical research facilities in a taut, glazed skin. The tower's base is composed of limestone and glass banding to balance and complement the College Wing. A future seventeen-storey tower along University Avenue will complete the final phase of the MaRS Centre.

Architect	**Adamson Associates | Architects**
Client	**MaRS Discovery District**
Completed	**Phase 1, 2005**
Address	**101 College Street**
Subway	**Yonge-University-Spadina Line, Queen's Park Station**
Streetcar	**506 Carlton**
Access	**atrium only**

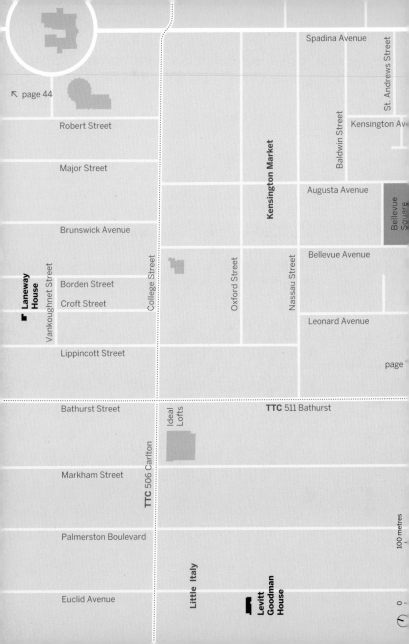

LITTLE ITALY / KENSINGTON MARKET

A visit to Toronto would not be complete without experiencing its charming residential neighbourhoods. Little Italy and Kensington Market are two fine examples within walking distance of the city centre. They also happen to contain two innovative examples of contemporary housing that are gaining popularity in Toronto: the infill house and the laneway house.

The fabled Kensington Market is a microcosm of Toronto's cultural diversity and has been declared a National Historic Site. The names of the streets allude to its history. Originally part of George Denison's large estate called Bellevue, it was subdivided into small plots for English and Irish workers. These homes became the backbone for succeeding waves of immigrants who would transform the neighbourhood, including European Jews who established the market in the early 20th century. The ground floors of homes were turned into the storefronts that would become a characteristic feature of this neighbourhood. Today, small family-run businesses still dominate the area and contribute to its strong social and artistic identity.

Extending west along College Street, Toronto's Little Italy is defined by its lively retail and sidewalk café culture. The neighbourhood attracted a large population of Italian immigrants after World War Two. While maintaining much of its Italian influence, the cultural landscape has expanded to include a strong Portuguese community and increased gentrification.

LEVITT GOODMAN HOUSE

This infill residential project proposes a contextual, sustainable and flexible solution to family living on a narrow 20-foot-wide lot. Well-scaled between two conventional houses, this modern insertion does not feel out of place in the streetscape.

Though the home is pristine and gallery-like, it offers a warm and inviting family environment. Large sliding doors encourage cross ventilation from the front to the back, while radiant slabs provide warmth to the concrete floors. Stretching through the ground floor, the long central island connects places for cooking, working and eating. A riserless stair allows daylight to pour from the central skylight to the two bedrooms on the basement level. Built to accommodate a single family, the home was designed to be easily divided into two residences by the conversion of the basement.

The second-floor master bedroom overlooks an ample green roof, whose native grasses, hosta and lavender can be seen from the street. The roof garden has the added benefits of keeping the building cool and managing stormwater.

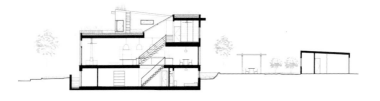

Architect	**Levitt Goodman Architects**
Landscape design	**Terry McGlade**
Client	**private**
Completed	**2006**
Address	**328 Euclid Avenue**
Streetcar	**506 Carlton**
Access	**private**

LANEWAY HOUSE

The cantilevered two-storey volume of dark brick and pigmented cement board signals that there is something out of the ordinary on this tiny site. This home is an exemplar of Toronto's modern laneway housing. Although Croft is technically a street, its lack of sidewalks, narrow width and continuous frontage of garages are characteristics of Toronto's service laneways.

The planning of the home maximizes both privacy on the ground floor and views from the second floor by inverting the typical relationship of a house. On the ground floor, the master bedroom and guest bedrooms have discreet views onto private outdoor spaces. On the second floor, the open-plan living spaces unfold like an airy tree house. Through large corner windows, diagonal views are provided of the city to the south and the neighbourhood to the north.

A powder room off the stair landing is neatly tucked under the counter of the kitchen above, and the open risers of the top-lit stairs allow light to permeate down to the basement. With its tiny floor plate, every inch of this home is designed with a purpose – and sometimes a dual purpose.

Architect	**Kohn Shnier Architects**
Client	**private**
Completed	**2004**
Address	**Croft Street, between Vankoughnet Street and Ulster Street**
Streetcar	**506 Carlton**
Access	**private**

↖ page 84

Peter Street

Blue Jays Way

District Lofts

401 Richmond

Clarence Square

TTC 510 Spadina

Spadina Avenue

Queen Street West

Richmond Street West

Camden Street

Adelaide Street West

King Street West

Wellington Street

Front Street West

Brant Street

St. Andrews Playground

TTC 504 King

Draper Street

Maud Street

← page 70

page 126

Portland Street

Evangel Hall

Stewart Street

Victoria Memorial Square Park

Twenty Niagara

TTC 511 Bathurst

Bathurst Street

Portugal Square

Niagara Street

100 metres

1 minute to walk

0

KING / SPADINA

Between 1833 and 1836, the area around Fort York, then known as the Garrison Reserve, was sold by the Crown to promote the city's western expansion. The established street grid of New Town was extended to create a residential district with numerous squares. Clarence Square and Victoria Square book-end Wellington Street, which was designed as a grand boulevard. Victoria Memorial Square Park, as it is now known, incorporates the site of the Garrison cemetery, where many men, women and children connected to Fort York were buried. The original residential character of the neighbourhood can still be experienced on Draper Street, which has been preserved as part of a Heritage Conservation District. Industrial pressures transformed this neighbourhood into a manufacturing area, composed of multi-storey brick warehouses.

As manufacturing was pushed offshore or to suburban locations, the district went into a period of decline. In the late 1990s, the implementation of a flexible planning framework enticed a wave of reinvestment in the area. The historic built form now accommodates a range of uses including restaurants, nightclubs, commercial and residential developments.

EVANGEL HALL

Evangel Hall is a prime example of a social housing project that successfully integrates the delivery of social services with high-calibre, thoughtful design. Within a modest budget, this sophisticated seven-storey building provides 84 transitional housing units as part of an inner city mission.

The building combines a single-room occupancy hotel and a social service hub. On the ground floor, a drop-in centre, cafeteria and other social services support the city's homeless. On the upper floors, modular residential units can be converted easily from studios to one and two-bedroom units.

Three distinct exterior masses interconnect and make clear their distinct functions. The western entrance leads to the social services wing, while the southern entrance acts as a lobby for the units above. A dark brick volume visually anchors the building and contains the common areas for resdents on each floor. With an occasional splash of lime green, a long narrow residential volume is clad in transparent and opaque glazing, masking this social housing development in the skin of a market condominium.

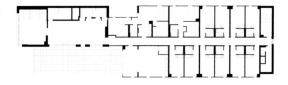

Architect **Regional Architects**
Landscape **Diana Gerrard Landscape Architecture**
Client **Presbyterian Church of Canada**
Completed **2006**
Address **552 Adelaide Street West**
Streetcar **511 Bathurst**
Access **lobby only**

TWENTY NIAGARA

This mid-rise condominium development hailed the beginning of the transformation of Toronto's urban housing market. The purchase of this small piece of land by Howard Cohen led to the founding of Context Development, which has been at the forefront of Toronto's residential condominium market. As the first of many collaborations between this developer and architect, Twenty Niagara demonstrated that there was an active desire for contemporary concrete and glass condominiums.

Situated directly on Victoria Memorial Square Park, the 22-unit slab building takes a fresh approach to the design of its units, circulation and safety. Replicating the typical front and back relationship found in houses, the through-units allow for cross-ventilation, extensive daylight and views. Internal corridors are eliminated by pairing two units to one elevator. In an inventive response to building code regulations, balconies are utilized as exit corridors in case of fire. These features have created an urbane, vertical neighbourhood, where a community is defined by the interdependency of its residents.

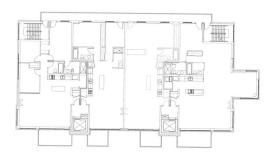

Architect	**architectsAlliance**
Landscape Architect	**James Floyd Landscape Architect**
Client	**Context Development**
Completed	**1998**
Address	**20 Niagara Street**
Streetcar	**511 Bathurst**
Access	**private**

DISTRICT LOFTS

Rising over the King / Spadina neighbourhood, the twin slabs of District Lofts signal an innovative residential building type. Born of a fruitful partnership between developer and architect, the fourteen-storey condominium is shoehorned into a tight site surrounded by 19th-century warehouse buildings.

The contextual brick base incorporates ground-floor retail and residential units, and conceals a raised parking garage. Atop this base, twinned slab towers employ an efficient skip-stop layout that creates two-storey through-units and minimizes corridor space. A central elevator tower clipped to the east end unifies the slabs, while dramatic exterior bridges connect the towers at the west end. The roofs slope towards an internal courtyard, forming a distinctive silhouette that stands out against the city's skyline.

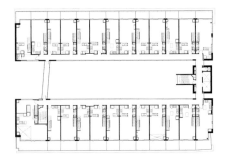

Architect	**architectsAlliance**
Client	**Context Development**
Completed	**2001**
Address	**338 Richmond Street West**
Streetcar	**510 Spadina**
Access	**private**

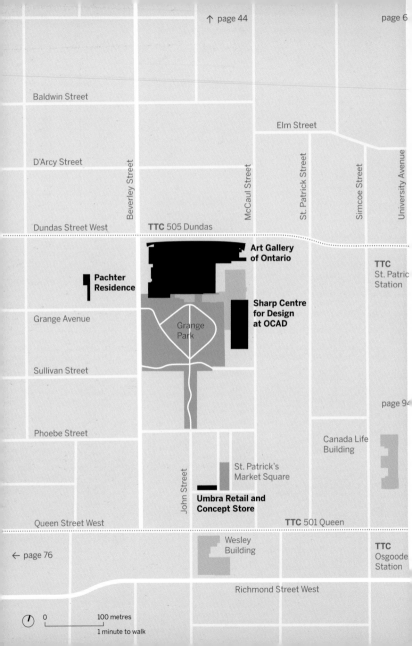

↑ page 44

page 6

Baldwin Street

Elm Street

D'Arcy Street

Beverley Street

McCaul Street

St. Patrick Street

Simcoe Street

University Avenue

Dundas Street West   **TTC** 505 Dundas

Art Gallery of Ontario

TTC St. Patric Station

Pachter Residence

Sharp Centre for Design at OCAD

Grange Avenue

Grange Park

Sullivan Street

page 94

Phoebe Street

Canada Life Building

John Street

St. Patrick's Market Square

Umbra Retail and Concept Store

Queen Street West   **TTC** 501 Queen

← page 76

Wesley Building

TTC Osgoode Station

Richmond Street West

0   100 metres
1 minute to walk

THE GRANGE

Once the centre of a large estate, The Grange is now a popular park. The handsome Georgian home along its northern edge was built by the successful dry-goods and general store owner, D'Arcy Boulton Jr., in 1817. As the city grew westward, Boulton sold much of his 100-acre property, defining the edges of Grange Park with the mansions that still line Beverley Street.

Over the 20th century, successive waves of immigrants moved through the neighbourhood engendering it with its multi-cultural character. Chinatown extends along Dundas Street West with diverse markets and restaurants that juxtapose the art galleries and student hangouts around the Ontario College of Art & Design.

To the south of Grange Park lies John Street with its fine examples of the adaptive reuse of warehouse buildings. Further south, the vibrancy of Queen Street West is anchored by the terracotta-clad Wesley building, home to pop culture television network MuchMusic.

Today, Grange Park acts as the foreground for two key protagonists in Toronto's architectural renaissance, the Sharp Centre and the Art Gallery of Ontario. This open space offers a unique vantage point to view the rapport between these two buildings.

UMBRA RETAIL AND CONCEPT STORE

For its first stand-alone retail outlet, Umbra, a worldwide leader in modern design products, wanted the architecture and retail design to be an icon in the city. The resulting three-storey building – clad in hot pink polycarbonate panels – makes a striking impression that attracts shoppers from Queen Street West.

In this adaptive reuse project, everything about the existing building has been reimagined. The existing steel frame was reused and the floor plates were cut to insert a double-height volume and a stepped ramp to the second floor. This wide ramp allows circulation and display areas to intermingle in a vitrine-like space overlooking John Street. The ground floor was extensively reglazed, allowing the pink extruded panels to act as a sunshade during the day and a lantern at night.

Architect	**Kohn Shnier Architects**
Interior Design	**Figure Three Interior Design**
Client	**Umbra**
Completed	**2007**
Address	**165 John Street**
Subway	**Yonge-University-Spadina Line, Osgoode Station**
Streetcar	**501 Queen**
Access	**public**

SHARP CENTRE FOR DESIGN AT ONTARIO COLLEGE OF ART & DESIGN

As British architect Will Alsop's first commission in North America, the Sharp Centre has garnered an enormous amount of attention for Toronto. The redevelopment of the Ontario College of Art & Design was aligned with both the aspirations of the Public Infrastructure Renewal program and the imagination of the critically acclaimed architect. In addition to public funding, a key donation was made by Rosalie Sharp, an alumna, and Isadore Sharp, founder of the Four Seasons Hotels.

The Sharp Centre takes advantage of a seemingly non-existent site that is surrounded by an eclectic community and Grange Park. The Tabletop, as it is affectionately known, is a two-storey studio building perched 85 feet in the air above the existing college, on angled, pencil crayon-like stilts. This design maintains views of the park for residents, adds open space at ground level, and is emblematic of the creative pedagogy of the college.

Day and night, colour is used as a dramatic device throughout the building. The black-and-white checkerboard cladding recedes to reveal fluorescent punched windows at night. Bold exterior lighting and lipstick pink slashes throughout the interior amplify the theatrical nature of the building.

Architect	**Alsop Architects / Robbie/Young + Wright Architects**
Structural Engineer	**Carruthers & Wallace Ltd.**
Landscape Architect	**YWLA**
Lighting Designer	**Stephen Pollard Lighting and Production Design**
Client	**Ontario College of Art & Design**
Completed	**2004**
Address	**100 McCaul Street**
Subway	**Yonge-University-Spadina Line, St. Patrick Station**
Streetcar	**505 Dundas**
Access	**college hours, www.ocad.ca**

THE GRANGE

ART GALLERY OF ONTARIO

Frank Gehry's transformation of the Art Gallery of Ontario (AGO) is a modest, disciplined example of infill and repair to an existing museum. Founded in 1900, the gallery has evolved through multiple expansions on this site, of which Transformation AGO is the latest. This was largely made possible through the philanthropy of Ken Thomson, who donated both substantial funding and his personal collection of Canadian and European art works to the redevelopment project.

Gehry's interventions are first evident on the exterior of the building. The billowing glass façade stretches the length of the block, reflecting the surrounding Victorian neighbourhood. The interior of the Galleria Italia provides a warm, linear exhibition space, which evokes the hull of ship laid on its side. The relocation of the main entrance to the centre of the Dundas Street West façade clarifies the relationship between the street, Walker Court and The Grange.

The lobby's serpentine ramp provides views to Ken Thomson's delightful model ship collection below, and leads patrons into the reimagined Walker Court. This 1920s-era court is the dramatic centre of the gallery. Its roof dissolves into a skylight with Douglas fir-clad stairs rising like a frozen plume of smoke, connecting to the blue titanium-clad tower above. The five-storey tower expansion provides well-scaled spaces for contemporary art, connected by twisting staircases that frame views of the city and Lake Ontario beyond.

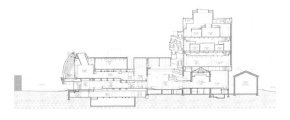

Architect	**Gehry Partners LLP / Adamson Associates ǀ Architects**
Heritage Architect	**ERA Architects**
Client	**Art Gallery of Ontario**
Completed	**2009**
Address	**317 Dundas Street West**
Subway	**Yonge-University-Spadina Line, St. Patrick Station**
Streetcar	**505 Dundas**
Access	**paid admission, www.ago.net**

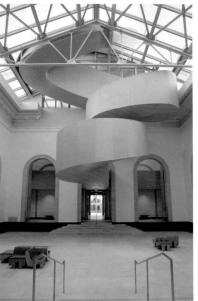

PACHTER RESIDENCE

Combining an artist's studio, a gallery and a living space, the Pachter Residence has a distilled material palette of glass and grey zinc that sets the home apart from its brick Victorian neighbours.

The residence is the result of a collaboration between the architect and the owner, well-known Canadian artist and art dealer Charles Pachter. They took advantage of the narrow site by stacking and staggering the program in a series of rectangular volumes. The spaces between these volumes allow for light to penetrate deep within the home and create opportunities for vertical circulation. Extensive windows frame views for the owner out to the neighbourhood, and allow a passerby glimpses into a private life.

Architect	**Teeple Architects**
Client	**Charles Pachter**
Completed	**2005**
Address	**22 Grange Avenue**
Streetcar	**505 Dundas**
Access	**private**

93

↑ page 62

↑ page

TTC Dundas Station

TTC St. Patrick Station

TTC 505 Dundas

Dundas Street

Yonge-Dundas Square

← page 84

Elizabeth Street

Toronto City Hall

Armoury Street

Trinity Square Park

Eaton Centre

Gould Street

Osgoode Hall

Nathan Phillips Square

Albert Street

TTC Osgoode Station

Old City Hall

Victoria Street

Bond Street

TTC 501 Queen

Queen Street East

Four Seasons Centre for the Performing Arts

TTC Queen Station

60 Richmon

Richmond Street East

Cloud Gardens

Temperance Street

Lombard Street

Bay Adelaide Centre

University Avenue

Adelaide Street West

Adelaide Street East

TTC St. Andrew Station

First Canadian Place

TTC King Station

Toronto Street

Courtho Square

King Street East

Commerce Court West

Toronto-Dominion Centre

Yonge Street

Scott Street

Leader Street

Wellington Street West

York Street

Fairmont Royal York

Bay Street

Allen Lambert Galleria

Berczy Park

Front Street

Station Street

TTC Union Station

The Esplanade

0   100 metres

1 minute to walk   ↓ page 126

DOWNTOWN / FINANCIAL DISTRICT

FOUR SEASONS CENTRE FOR THE PERFORMING ARTS
ALLEN LAMBERT GALLERIA, BROOKFIELD PLACE
50 RICHMOND
YONGE-DUNDAS SQUARE

New Town is the original name for this area first developed in the late 19th century as the westward expansion of the Old Town of York. It began as a low-rise, mixed commercial and residential district. The Great Fire of 1904 destroyed much of the area, creating an opportunity for Toronto's first skyscraper to be erected at 1 King Street East. Though numerous skyscrapers were built in the first half of the 20th century, post-World War II steel and glass skyscrapers constructed by prominent financial institutions now define this district.

The Toronto-Dominion Centre, designed by Mies Van der Rohe, is the finest example of the International Style in Toronto. Two original towers and a one-storey bank hall readily demonstrate the powerful juxtaposition of a tower and a plaza. Directly to the north is Edward Durell Stone's First Canadian Place, originally clad in sumptuous white Carrara marble. Further east, Commerce Court is a composition of four office towers, created when the 1930s Darling & Pearson skyscraper was integrated with I.M. Pei's modern Commerce Court West.

In 1992, the Santiago Calatrava-designed Allen Lambert Galleria opened as part of BCE Place. This development marked the apex of the late 20th century skyscraper period in Toronto. As the recession of the early 1990s crept in, other projects ground to a halt, most famously the Bay-Adelaide Centre. Locally nicknamed the Stump, this six-storey unfinished building core stood as a gash in the city for two decades until it was demolished in 2007 for the construction of the new Bay-Adelaide Centre.

FOUR SEASONS CENTRE FOR THE PERFORMING ARTS

Three decades in the making, the Four Seasons Centre for the Performing Arts is Toronto's long-awaited home to the Canadian Opera Company and the National Ballet of Canada. The design and program evolved through multiple sites, architects and iterations before the current facility was realized – largely due to the tenacity of the late Richard Bradshaw, director of the Canadian Opera Company.

Bound on four sides by busy streets and located above the subway, the site posed many technical and programmatic challenges for the design of a performance space. Though the building has been criticized for its lack of urban relationships on three of its sides, the corner of University Avenue and Queen Street West is active and engaging, most notably on performance nights.

Framed by a clear curtain of glazing, the theatrical spectacle is perhaps best exemplified by the City Room and amphitheatre overlooking University Avenue. Glass stairs and mezzanines intertwine in this four-storey space, where seeing and being seen is all part of the performance.

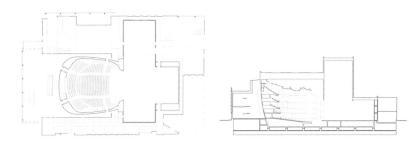

Architect	**Diamond + Schmitt Architects**
Landscape Architect	**du Toit Allsopp Hillier**
Client	**Canadian Opera Company Corporation**
Completed	**2006**
Address	**145 Queen Street West**
Subway	**Yonge-University-Spadina Line, Osgoode Station**
Streetcar	**501 Queen**
Access	**paid admission, www.coc.ca**

DOWNTOWN / FINANCIAL DISTRICT

ALLEN LAMBERT GALLERIA, BROOKFIELD PLACE

Designed as part of Brookfield Place (formerly known as BCE Place), the Allen Lambert Galleria is the result of a public art competition supported by funds generated through the increased densities permitted on the site. Santiago Calatrava's sculptural insertion compelled the developers to devote the entire public art fund to the creation of the galleria. This privately owned public space utilizes public art to elevate a pedestrian passageway into a cathedral-like experience.

The six-storey galleria and Sam Pollack Heritage Square form a glazed connection between Bay Street and Yonge Street. From the entrance on Bay Street, the inclined steel columns leap skyward to form a graceful, treelike structure supporting a glazed canopy. The arches march rhythmically along the 350-foot length of the galleria, casting alternating patterns of light and shadow.

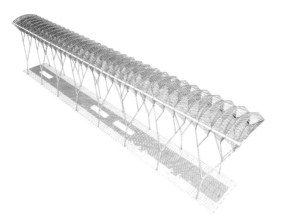

Architect	**B+H Architects**
Designer	**Santiago Calatrava**
Client	**Brookfield Development Corporation**
Completed	**1992**
Address	**181 Bay Street**
Subway	**Yonge-University-Spadina Line, Union Station**
Bus	**6 Bay**
Access	**public**

60 RICHMOND

The 60 Richmond project develops a sustainable, self-sufficient agricultural and cultural ecosystem for its residents, in an urbane affordable rental housing development.

While searching for potential residents with shared interests, the Toronto Community Housing Corporation proposed a strategy to house those temporarily displaced by the Regent Park Revitalization project. From this initiative, it was discovered that many were members of the same union and worked in the hospitality industry – all in downtown Toronto. A unique program to accommodate these residents was conceived for a site close to downtown. The residential program was expanded to include a restaurant, a teaching kitchen and an outdoor vegetable garden.

Large volumes are carved out of the building's mass to create a ten-storey lightwell and a sixth-floor garden to grow herbs and vegetables for the restaurant. A green roof collects water to irrigate this garden, while compost from the kitchen restores nutrients to the soil.

Architect	**Teeple Architects**
Landscape Architect	**NAK Design**
Client	**Toronto Community Housing Corporation**
Completed	**2009**
Address	**60 Richmond Street East**
Subway	**Yonge-University-Spadina Line, Queen Station**
Streetcar	**501 Queen**
Access	**private**

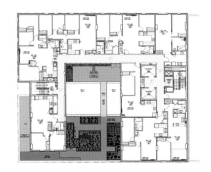

YONGE-DUNDAS SQUARE

In contrast with Toronto's verdant parks, Yonge-Dundas Square is an urban piazza framed by commercial activity and striking billboards. Selected as the winning scheme in a two-stage international competition in 1998, the square is the result of a successful partnership between the City and the Downtown Yonge Business Improvement Area Association to rejuvenate a district that was in decline.

The distinctive, bulging ground plane is clad in a tartan pattern of black and green granite. A zinc-and-wood canopy skirts the northern edge of the square, providing a sense of enclosure from Dundas Street. In the south-east corner, the granite surface peels up to create a stage, while screening the entrance to the parking garage below. A double row of concealed water geysers encourages play and offers cool relief to all ages.

Yonge-Dundas Square challenges Torontonians' traditional perception of open space both through its conception as a hard surface plaza, and operation as a privately managed public space.

Architect	**Brown + Storey Architects**
Client	**City of Toronto, Downtown Yonge Business Improvement Area Association**
Completed	**2002**
Address	**1 Dundas Street East**
Subway	**Yonge-University-Spadina Line, Dundas Station**
Streetcar	**505 Dundas**
Access	**public**

← page 26

Isabella Street

St. James Town

Gloucester Street

Dundonald Street

**Wellesley
Community
Centre**

TTC
Wellesley Station

Wellesley Street East **TTC** 94 Wellesley

Maitland Street

Alexander Street

Mutual Strret

Homewood Avenue

Bleecker Steet

**Canada's
National
Ballet
School**

Wood Street Maple Leaf
Gardens

TTC
College Station

Radiocity

Carlton Street

TTC 506 Carlton

Church Street

Allan
Gardens

← page 62

Gerrard Street East

Ryerson
University
Quad

Gould Street

Jarvis Street

George Street

Pembroke Street

Sherbourne Street

↙ page 94

TTC
Dundas
Station

Devonian
Square

Yonge-Dundas
Square

Dundas Street East

TTC 505 Dundas

Yonge Street

0   100 metres
1 minute to walk

JARVIS / WELLESLEY

As one of the oldest developed parts of the city, Jarvis / Wellesley is a collection of distinct neighbourhoods. Formerly home to the estates of Toronto's leading families, this area was developed in the 19th century into one of the most fashionable parts of town. Though poor land use and transportation planning stripped Jarvis Street and St. James Town of much of their original character, ongoing community initiatives are helping to rejuvenate these areas.

Once lined with beautiful mansions, lush verges and tall trees, Jarvis Street has become a major north-south automobile thoroughfare in the city. At the height of Toronto's Victorian and Edwardian periods, Jarvis Street was the address of prominent families such as the Cawthras, the Masseys and industrialist George Gooderham. The character of Jarvis Street changes almost block by block, as it connects the neighbourhoods of St. Lawrence Market, Moss Park, the eastern edge of Ryerson University, Allan Gardens and the Church and Wellesley Village.

Formerly a middle-class area, St. James Town was razed by developers in the 1950s to create a high-rise residential apartment community. Today, it is one of Canada's most densely populated and culturally diverse neighbourhoods. The low-rent apartment towers are often the first home to new immigrants in Toronto, although they offer few amenities to residents. The recent construction of the Wellesley Community Centre attempts to address this need.

RADIOCITY

Radiocity represents a model of development that uses residential condominiums as a vehicle to support a cultural project. After purchasing the
former site of the Canadian Broadcasting Corporation (CBC), Context
Development put together a deal that sold the historic buildings and
roughly half of the land to Canada's National Ballet School for $1. This
transaction transferred development densities from the former CBC site
to the Radiocity site, enabling the expansion of the National Ballet School
while making the Radiocity development financially feasible.

The resulting high-rise condominium towers and townhomes are situated
to form landscaped courtyards that connect to the new National Ballet
School. The towers are set back from the street edge, and their lightness
and transparency is accentuated by their small footprints. The handsome
townhomes maintain the residential scale of the adjacent neighbourhood
while defining the edge of this new community.

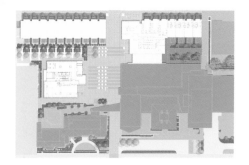

Architect	**architectsAlliance**
Urban Design	**Urban Strategies**
Public Artist	**Roland Brener**
Client	**Context Development**
Completed	**2006**
Address	**281–285 Mutual Street**
Subway	**Yonge-University-Spadina Line, College Station**
Streetcar	**506 Carlton**
Access	**private**

CANADA'S NATIONAL BALLET SCHOOL

Canada's National Ballet School is one of Toronto's key Cultural Renaissance projects. It is the result of a careful orchestration of private development and cultural reinvestment, philanthropic and public funding, and heritage and contemporary architecture. Stage 1 of Project Grand Jeté organized a vertical campus expansion on a tight site, incorporating heritage buildings in a seemingly effortless manner.

As North America's only institute to offer an integrated program of professional dance training, advanced academics and dormitory living space, the school's spatial requirements necessitated a vertical stacking of dance studios above academic and amenity space. The Celia Franca Centre's six-storey glazed curtain wall on Jarvis Street reveals studios where dancers are onstage with the city as a backdrop. Forming the heart of the school, the three-storey Town Square visually and socially connects the heritage Northfield House to the rest of the facility.

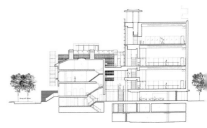

Architect	**Kuwabara Payne McKenna Blumberg Architects & Goldsmith Borgal and Company Limited Architects**
Landscape Architect	**The MBTW Group**
Urban Planners	**Urban Strategies**
Client	**Canada's National Ballet School**
Completed	**2005**
Address	**400 Jarvis Street**
Subway	**Yonge-University-Spadina Line, College Station**
Streetcar	**506 Carlton**
Access	**lobby only**

WELLESLEY COMMUNITY CENTRE

Sited at the south-west corner of St. James Town, the Wellesley Community Centre knits together a diverse community. Despite being one of the most densely populated areas in Canada, St. James Town previously lacked community amenities. The new facility combines a public library, a gym, a daycare and community rooms in what has become a cultural centre for many new Canadians.

Entrances from both Sherbourne Street and Bleecker Street create a spacious double-sided lobby that connects the St. James Town community to the surrounding neighbourhood. Robust exterior finishes of brick and precast concrete are enlivened by colourful stucco and mosaic tile, while the stained concrete block and glass tile of the interior are washed in a diffused light from skylights.

Architect	**MacLennan Jaunkalns Miller Architects / ZAS Architects**
Landscape Architect	**Gunta Mackars Landscape Architecture**
Client	**City of Toronto and Toronto Public Library**
Completed	**2007**
Address	**495 Sherbourne Street**
Subway	**Yonge-University-Spadina Line, Wellesley Station**
Bus	**94 Wellesley**
Access	**public**

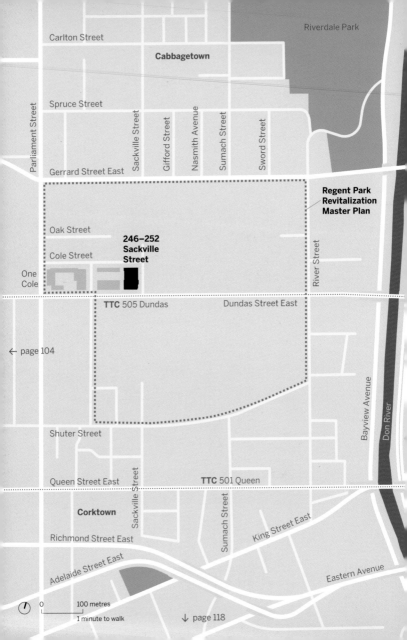

Carlton Street

Cabbagetown

Riverdale Park

Spruce Street

Parliament Street

Sackville Street

Gifford Street

Nasmith Avenue

Sumach Street

Sword Street

Gerrard Street East

**Regent Park
Revitalization
Master Plan**

Oak Street

Cole Street

**246–252
Sackville
Street**

River Street

One
Cole

TTC 505 Dundas

Dundas Street East

← page 104

Bayview Avenue

Don River

Shuter Street

Queen Street East

Sackville Street

TTC 501 Queen

Corktown

Sumach Street

King Street East

Richmond Street East

Adelaide Street East

Eastern Avenue

0   100 metres
1 minute to walk

↓ page 118

REGENT PARK

Regent Park occupies an area where South Cabbagetown once stood. In an act of misguided urban renewal, the notorious slums were razed in the 1940s to create Canada's first and largest social housing project.

Occupying 69 acres of land, the project's original plan has been much maligned for its lack of connections to the city's street grid, underutilized green space and the absence of street-related retail, which was not uncommon for social housing of this era.

Over the past fifty years, Regent Park has grown into one of Toronto's most culturally diverse communities, with a high number of immigrants and with over half the population under the age of eighteen. While it was initially designed as a transitional solution, it has developed into a permanent community despite the challenges imposed by the social design philosophy of its planners.

REGENT PARK REVITALIZATION MASTER PLAN

Sparked by the need to renew over fifty-year-old infrastructure, Toronto Community Housing Corporation completed the Regent Park Revitalization Master Plan to sustainably redevelop and reintegrate the community into its surrounding neighbourhood.

The master plan restores the former street pattern and redevelops residential properties in a mix of affordable and market-rate dwellings. Street-related development replaces the tower-in-the-park typology of the previous 1950s era plan. Ground-floor spaces will provide opportunities for employment and education, as well as cultural and community facilities. Most important, the master plan calls for the transformation of Regent Park into a mixed-income residential community, to end the segregation of Toronto's urban poor without displacing them.

The $1 billion redevelopment will take up to a decade to complete. The first phase is currently underway, including the Regent Park Community Energy System that will provide heating, cooling and hot water to buildings while reducing greenhouse gases. The second phase will see the construction of a new central park and aquatics facility.

Design Team **GHK International / Ken Greenberg Consultants / Markson Borooah Hodgson Architects / David Millar Associates / Dillon Consulting Ltd. / Jim Ward Associates / Envision the Hough Group**
Client **Toronto Community Housing Corporation**
Completed **in progress**
Address **Parliament Street to River Street, Gerrard Street East to Shuter Street**
Streetcar **505 Dundas**
Access **public**

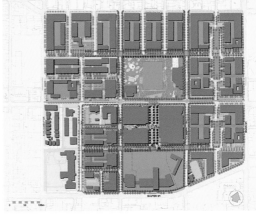

246–252 SACKVILLE STREET

This complex was the winning design of an invited architectural competition held by Toronto Community Housing Corporation (TCHC) to kick off redevelopment of Regent Park. The competition promoted TCHC's commitment to mixed-income communities and sustainable design. It also marked the formation of its Design Review Panel, which is charged with maintaining design excellence in the redevelopment of this community, its facilities and its spaces.

Showcasing some of the most spectacular views in the city, 252 Sackville is a refinement of the architect's exploration of the language of the point tower. Rising twenty-two storeys, this seniors-oriented tower skilfully incorporates rental units, an amenity space and a community energy system plant that will service a majority of the neighbourhood in a seamless composition. With its rooftop garden, the eight-storey, 246 Sackville is a family-oriented building with two- to three-bedroom units overlooking Dundas Street East. This affordable-housing development uses high quality materials and contemporary design, making it virtually indistinguishable from its market-rate condominium neighbour.

Architect	**architectsAlliance**
Client	**Toronto Community Housing Corporation**
Completed	**2009**
Address	**246–252 Sackville Street**
Streetcar	**505 Dundas**
Access	**private**

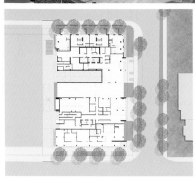

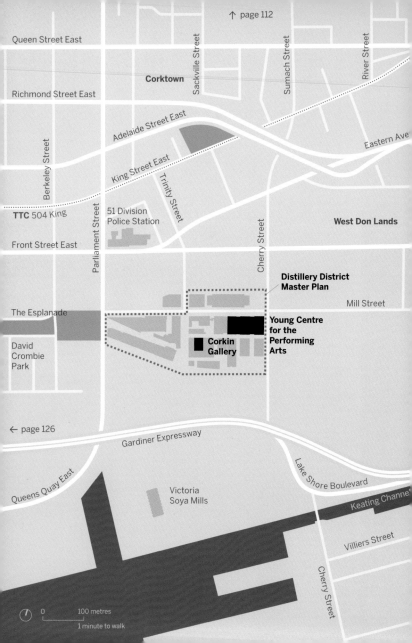

↑ page 112

Queen Street East

Corktown

Richmond Street East

Adelaide Street East

Sackville Street

Sumach Street

River Street

Eastern Ave

King Street East

Berkeley Street

Trinity Street

TTC 504 King

51 Division
Police Station

Cherry Street

West Don Lands

Front Street East

Parliament Street

**Distillery District
Master Plan**

Mill Street

The Esplanade

**Young Centre
for the
Performing
Arts**

■ **Corkin
Gallery**

David
Crombie
Park

← page 126

Gardiner Expressway

Lake Shore Boulevard

Queens Quay East

Victoria
Soya Mills

Keating Channel

Villiers Street

Cherry Street

0   100 metres

1 minute to walk

OLD TOWN TORONTO

The area referred to as Old Town today encompasses such neighbour-hoods as Corktown, West Don Lands, Distillery District, St. Lawrence Neighbourhood and the former Town of York. Established in 1793, the original ten blocks of the Town of York were surveyed along King Street between Jarvis Street and Ontario Street. This area also includes the site of Upper Canada's first Parliament Buildings, built in 1794 and destroyed by American troops in 1813.

Home to workers from the nearby distilleries, breweries and brickyards, Corktown was nicknamed after the home county of its Irish residents. Vestiges of the original rowhouses can still be found, but many were demol-ished in the development of Toronto's arterial road system.

The Distillery District is one of the best-preserved collections of Victorian era industrial architecture in North America. It is the birthplace of Canada's oldest distillery, Gooderham and Worts, which began as a flour mill on the waterfront, building a still in 1837 to produce spirits for the burgeoning Town of York. Within ten years, it was the largest distillery in the British Empire. Over the 20th century, its production slowly waned until 1990 when operations ceased. Today, this red-brick-paved district is an emerging arts-focused neighbourhood.

To the immediate east and north of the Distillery District, the West Don Lands neighbourhood is planned to include nearly 6,000 residential units in a pedestrian-friendly mixed-use district. Work has already begun on the future Don River Park and several adjacent developments. This new residential area will reinforce a much-needed connection between the Distillery District and the surrounding neighbourhoods.

DISTILLERY DISTRICT MASTER PLAN

After the Gooderham and Worts distillery closed its doors in 1990, the area fell derelict for a decade and seemed resistant to development. In 2001, the complex was purchased by Cityscape to transform the 13-acre industrial site and its 44 buildings – including the large stone distillery, brick malthouse, kilns and warehouses – into a pedestrian-oriented arts, culture and entertainment district, just east of Toronto's downtown.

Today, the historic character of the red-brick, stone and green painted wood and steel still informs the material palette of the buildings and the public realm. The area has been carefully curated and revitalized as an active commercial and residential community set amongst 19th-century industrial buildings.

The consistency of architectural style and occupation of the spaces in between the buildings lend the site a charm found nowhere else in Toronto. The district is also home to many excellent examples of the adaptive reuse of heritage structures, such as the Corkin Gallery and the Young Centre for the Performing Arts. New mixed-use buildings like the Pure Spirit condominium demonstrate that bold contemporary architecture can also be contextual.

Coordinating Architect	**ERA Architects**
Contributing Architectural Team	**architectsAlliance / Studio Andrea Bruno / Roger du Toi**
	Architects / Fercon Architects / Kohn Shnier Architects
	Kuwabara Payne McKenna Blumberg Architects /
	Quadrangle Architects Ltd. / Shim-Sutcliffe Architects
	Zeidler Partnership
Client	**Cityscape Holdings Inc. and Dundee Realty Corporation**
Completed	**opened 2003, in progress**
Address	**Parliament Street and Mill Street**
Streetcar	**504 King**
Access	**public**

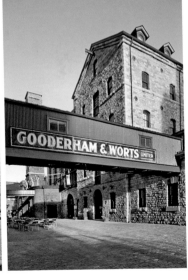

CORKIN GALLERY

The Corkin Gallery is an adaptive reuse project where contemporary design is employed to highlight existing heritage qualities. Housed in a space originally used for the manufacture and storage of distilled spirits, the gallery is created by a precise incision into the heritage structure, revealing a robust sculptural landscape.

The gallery experience is one of long sightlines and the discovery of intimate spaces. Rows of brick piers define the top-lit main volume of the gallery. Evocative steel bases support the original wood columns and denote the former floor level creating a dialogue between new and existing structural elements. Beneath the mezzanine, catacomb-like spaces recall the service passageways that once ran beneath the vats of spirits. Steel and wood stairs ascend to the mezzanine level, where an office and library are screened behind planes of steel and sandblasted glass. From the mezzanine, a catwalk connects the smaller galleries and allows the visitor a new perspective across the gallery.

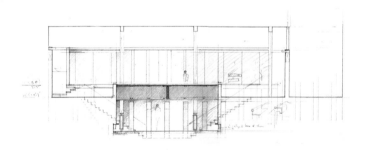

Architect	**Shim-Sutcliffe Architects**
Heritage Architect	**ERA Architects**
Client	**Corkin Shopland Gallery**
Completed	**2005**
Address	**55 Mill Street, Building 61**
Streetcar	**504 King**
Access	**public**

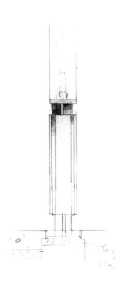

YOUNG CENTRE FOR THE PERFORMING ARTS

The Young Centre for the Performing Arts illustrates the richness that can occur when old buildings are used as containers for new ideas. Housed in – and inserted between – Tank Houses 4, 9 and 10, this collaborative centre was created when Soulpepper Theatre and George Brown College joined their theatre company and teaching program. This adaptive reuse project links three background warehouse structures through the insertion of a lobby and reception space animated by theatre-goers and students.

The discreet projection of a metal canopy draws pedestrians down Tank House Lane into the theatre. The patina of the existing masonry acts as a backdrop for the dramatic rough-hewn timber trusses that define this new lobby space. Housing a café, box office and bar, this inspired in-between space expresses the simplicity and economy of the scheme.

Architect **Kuwabara Payne McKenna Blumberg Architects**
Heritage Architect **ERA Architects**
Client **George Brown College and Soulpepper Theatre Compan**
Completed **2006**
Address **55 Mill Street, Building 49**
Streetcar **504 King**
Access **paid admission, www.youngcentre.ca**

OLD TOWN TORONTO

↑ page 118

Yonge Street

Bay Street

← page 94

Air Canada Centre

Gardiner Expressway

Lakeshore Boulevard

Queens Quay West

TTC Union Station

York Street

Toronto Harbour

Bremner Boulevard

Simcoe Street

The Roundhouse

TTC 509 Harbourfront

Simcoe WaveDeck

Harbourfront Centre

Front Street West

CN Tower

Rees Street

Rees WaveDeck

Rogers Centre

Blue Jays Way

HTO Park

Spadina WaveDeck

Spadina Avenue

TTC 510 Spadina

← page 76

Toronto Music Garden

Portland Street

Toronto Island Airport

Canada Malting Silos

Ireland Park

Bathurst Street

TTC 511 Bathurst

Central Waterfront Master Plan

Stadium Road

Fort York

200 metres

0

THE WATERFRONT

The railway lines, elevated expressways and arterial boulevards that run parallel to the shoreline have created a physical and psychological barrier to the waterfront. Lying in wait on the far side of this inhospitable infrastructure is one of Toronto's most remarkable and under-appreciated areas. Though once characterized by the smokestacks of industry, the waterfront today is being reclaimed for the public and transforming into a thriving community.

Successive industrial plans have reshaped the water's edge, as various lake-filling activities have moved the shoreline from its natural location near Front Street to its current location, nearly a kilometre to the south. At present, the area is characterized by a series of imposing but nondescript residential developments along an incongruous public realm. Bright spots such as Harbourfront Centre, a multi-disciplinary artistic, cultural and entertainment complex, as well as HTO Park, the Toronto Music Garden and Ireland Park are providing many incentives to come down to the waterfront.

Most recently, the federal, provincial and municipal governments established Waterfront Toronto, an arm's-length agency tasked with overseeing and spearheading waterfront renewal. With sustainable development and design excellence as two of its guiding principles, the agency is promoting an agenda of building parks, public realm and transit in advance of development. Following the success of three recent international design competitions and numerous public realm components scheduled for completion in the coming years, anticipation is replacing the cynicism that tends to run high in a city that has seen many waterfront plans come and go.

CENTRAL WATERFRONT MASTER PLAN

Inspired by the iconography and rugged landscape of Canada, a joint Dutch-Canadian team reimagined what an urban Canadian waterfront could be. As the winning submission for a 2006 international design competition, the master plan proposes a vision to connect the city to the water through strategic interventions that create a unifying identity while reinforcing existing public spaces along the waterfront. The designers' love of the Canadian lakefront is evident in their choice of materials, including heavy timber and granite, and in their use of an abstract maple leaf mosaic pattern throughout.

As Toronto's main waterfront street, Queens Quay will be transformed into a grand pedestrian-friendly boulevard featuring a linear park on the south side with a generous tree-lined promenade and multi-use trail. The north side of the street offers improved streetcar accessibility and fewer lanes of traffic. A granite promenade and wooden boardwalks, along with a series of wavedecks and pedestrian bridges spanning the ends of the slips, will create new types of public space, providing continuous access to the water's edge.

The Central Waterfront Master Plan is a work in progress, with construction of many of its features currently underway.

Master Plan Team	**West 8 + DTAH / Halsall Associates / Schollen & Company / Arup / David Dennis Design / (Diamond + Schmitt Architects, McCormick Rankin Corporation – competition team only)**
Client	**Waterfront Toronto**
Completed	**in progress**
Address	**Queens Quay West, from Bathurst Street to Parliament Street**
Streetcar	**509 Harbourfront**
Access	**public**

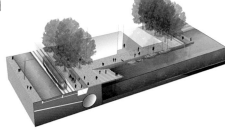

THE WATERFRONT

SPADINA, REES & SIMCOE WAVEDECKS

As the first constructed elements of the Central Waterfront Master Plan, the Spadina, Rees and Simcoe WaveDecks provide a new type of public space for Toronto. Previously pinch points along a sidewalk, these decks span the heads of the slips and create various opportunities for active and passive interactions with the water's edge. The structures of ipe wood and yellow cedar resemble the natural contours of the Canadian landscape and shelter an extensive fish habitat beneath their wooden decks.

The Spadina WaveDeck is a gently bulging promontory over the water's edge. Spanning a boat slip at the foot of Spadina Avenue, it elegantly stitches together the Toronto Music Garden and the western portion of HTO Park.

The Rees WaveDeck is an informal amphitheatre stepping down to the water. Designed in part for the small crafts and boating clubs in the slip, it lets the public engage with Lake Ontario in a novel way.

The Simcoe WaveDeck is a dynamic rippling form reflecting the energy of Harbourfront Centre. A railing snakes along the side of the steep, undulating slopes that children have appropriated into a slide.

Architect	**West 8 + DTAH**
Client	**Waterfront Toronto**
Completed	**Spadina WaveDeck: 2008,**
	Rees WaveDeck and Simcoe WaveDeck: 2009
Address	**Queens Quay West, between Spadina Avenue**
	and Simcoe Street
Streetcar	**509 Harbourfront**
Access	**public**

HTO PARK

The winning submission in a 2003 design competition, HTO Park (H_2O+TO) reconnects the city to the water's edge in an overtly artificial landscape. A positive step in the reclamation of the waterfront for residents, the park's completion was not without obstacles. In addition to the physical challenges posed by an aging dockwall and the site's industrial past, the key challenge was to alter perceptions of how an active inner harbour can coexist with a publicly accessible waterfront.

The Peter Street Slip divides the site into two parcels. A playful topography of island-like dunes lined with meandering pathways provides a separation from traffic while inviting visitors to enjoy the waterfront under the shade of silver maple and willow trees. Bright yellow beach umbrellas are planted in a defined, man-made beach, creating a surreal landscape. Framed by generous slab-like benches, a wooden boardwalk skirts along the water's edge where the harbour stretches out on the watery stage before you.

Landscape Architect	**Janet Rosenberg + Associates /**
	Claude Cormier Architectes Paysagistes
Architect	**Hariri Pontarini Architects**
Client	**City of Toronto**
Completed	**2007**
Address	**339 Queens Quay West**
Streetcar	**509 Harbourfront or 510 Spadina**
Access	**public**

TORONTO MUSIC GARDEN

The Toronto Music Garden is an enchanting 3-acre park that packs a variety of experiences into a garden whose story is as interesting as the design itself. The park is the result of a successful collaboration between famed cellist Yo-Yo Ma and landscape architect Julie Moir Messervy.

It was originally planned for Boston's City Hall Plaza, but the cancellation of that project led to its resurrection on Toronto's waterfront. The collective will of key officials and patrons drew together the designers, the site and the funding to make the park a reality. Ma and Messervy were brought to Toronto to tour the site and witness its dedication by City Council. That evening's performance by Ma and the Toronto Symphony Orchestra culminated in a pledge by the former director of the Art Gallery of Ontario, James Douglas Fleck, to raise the capital funding needed for the construction of the park.

Based on the first suite of Bach's Six Suites for Unaccompanied Cello, the design has successfully grown into a series of well-articulated outdoor rooms that convey the mood and emotion of music through landscape. The amphitheatre, the arbour and the maypole are key spaces along the curving path that winds through thick conifers, lush ornamental grasses and wildflower meadows.

Landscape Architect	**Julie Moir Messervy and City of Toronto Department of Parks and Recreation**
Artistic Consultant	**Yo-Yo Ma**
Client	**City of Toronto**
Completed	**1999**
Address	**475 Queens Quay West**
Streetcar	**509 Harbourfront or 510 Spadina**
Access	**public**

IRELAND PARK

Tucked behind the derelict Canada Malting Silos, Ireland Park is an evocative space that captures the intertwining of life, death and memory. Planned for over eleven years before opening on the waterfront, this park is a memorial to the Irish immigrants who fled the famine in Ireland, finally disembarking in Toronto in 1847. Championed by the local Irish community, the park occupies a site not far from where many Irish immigrants first landed.

The dark towering cliff of stacked stone forms a rugged artificial landscape reminiscent of the shores of Ireland. Crevices in this Kilkenny limestone reveal the almost forgotten names of those who died while fleeing the famine. Five bronze figures by sculptor Rowan Gillespie convey an overwhelming sense of anguish. These haunting figures symbolically face east towards a reciprocal memorial on the River Liffey in Dublin, Ireland.

Architect	**Kearns Mancini Architects**
Sculptor	**Rowan Gillespie**
Client	**City of Toronto**
Completed	**2007**
Address	**5 Eirann Quay, foot of Bathurst Street**
Streetcar	**509 Harbourfront or 511 Bathurst**
Access	**public**

Rouge River

Thomas
L. Wells
Public
School

Scarborough
Chinese
Baptist Church

Lake
Ontario

Don Valley Expressway

Claude
Watson
School for
the Arts

Toronto
Botanical
Garden

Bloorview
Kids
Rehab

CNIB
Centre

Don River

Schulich
School of
Business

Highway 401

Gardiner Expressway

Humber River
Bicycle and Pedestrian
Bridge

Highway 400

Eatonville
Public Library

Highway 427

Terminal 1,
Toronto Pearson
International
Airport

Etobicoke Creek

Queen Elizabeth Way

0   2000 metres

POST-AMALGAMATION TORONTO

In 1998, the Province of Ontario amalgamated the six municipalities comprising Metropolitan Toronto: East York, Etobicoke, North York, Scarborough, York, and the former City of Toronto. This amalgamation, enacted as a cost-saving measure, was opposed by the majority of municipal politicians and citizens, who nicknamed the new conglomerate "The MegaCity."

Now the fifth largest city in North America, Toronto continues to reconcile the political, social and cultural differences between the former city and its amalgamated municipalities. All across Toronto, thriving ethnic communities are emerging, as exemplified by the parish of the Scarborough Chinese Baptist Church.

Bound on the east by the Rouge River and on the west by Etobicoke Creek, the landscape of the city is defined by its dramatic ravines and watersheds. Though the downtown is deceptively flat, a varied topography is most evident in the Scarborough Bluffs, the Don Valley and many other ravine parks, such as the Edward Gardens at the Toronto Botanical Garden.

HUMBER RIVER BICYCLE AND PEDESTRIAN BRIDGE

Unofficially recognized as the western gateway to Toronto, the Humber River Bicycle and Pedestrian Bridge boldly arcs across the river and connects trails between Etobicoke and Toronto. The bridge was built by Metro Toronto Transportation as part of the redevelopment of the highway infrastructure spanning the river. Its soaring tubular arches with their stainless-steel hangers create both a destination along the waterfront and a promontory from which to view the city's skyline.

The inclined supports of the tied-arch bridge narrow towards the top where they are skillfully woven together with a cut-out Thunderbird motif, recalling the importance of this river in Ojibwa society. Interestingly, the bridge was erected on the banks of the Humber before being floated across and hoisted into place fully assembled.

Architect	**Montgomery Sisam Architects**
Landscape Architect	**Ferris & Quinn Associates Inc.**
Engineers	**Delcan Corporation**
Public Artist	**Environmental Artworks Studio**
Client	**Municipality of Metropolitan Toronto Transportation Department**
Completed	**1996**
Address	**Humber River at Lake Ontario**
Streetcar	**501 Queen or 508 Lakeshore**
Access	**public**

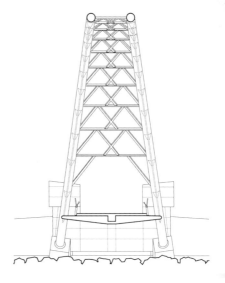

EATONVILLE PUBLIC LIBRARY

At the juncture of a highway and a residential neighbourhood, the Eatonville Public Library successfully responds to the contrasting nature of its context and provides a well-loved community resource.

The zinc band that wraps the east and south elevations has the cool crispness of a machine-made element, while the stone wall to the north reflects the residential nature of Burnhamthorpe Drive. At the corner, a community room is defined by the intersection of these two façades. The main volume of the library is shaped by a folding ceiling element that hovers above the circulation desk, allowing north light to pour through clerestory windows. Niches and bay windows along the rows of stacks define small study spaces, while a low window with a generous sill allows children to watch the activity of the street beyond.

Architect	**Teeple Architects**
Client	**Toronto Public Library**
Completed	**2000**
Address	**430 Burnhamthorpe Road**
Transit	**Bloor-Danforth Line, Kipling Station, bus 111 East Mall**
Access	**public**

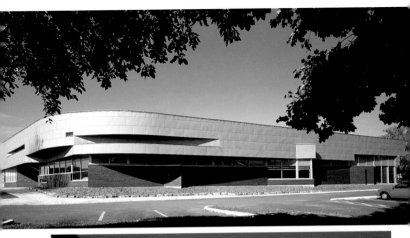

TERMINAL 1,
TORONTO PEARSON INTERNATIONAL AIRPORT

Constructed as the first phase of a $4.4 billion redevelopment of Toronto's Pearson International Airport, Terminal 1 is the flagship of Canada's largest and busiest airport.

Covering over 4 million square feet, Terminal 1 is a bold curvilinear space under an arched roof that spans 250 feet. Glass bridges connect the departure hall to secure areas, allowing daylight to penetrate into the baggage level below. The Terminal is naturally lit, revealing the structure in muted grey and white tones, punctuated by colourful pieces from the airport's extensive art collection. Sited in strategic locations, these works of art animate spaces and provide delight for travellers while also serving as informal way-finding devices. These commissioned pieces form part of a permanent collection acquired by the GTAA.

Architect	**Airports Architects Canada, a joint venture of Skidmore Owings & Merrill Ltd., Adamson Associates | Architects, and Moshe Safdie and Associates**
Structural Engineers	**ARUP, Yolles Partnership Ltd.**
Client	**Greater Toronto Airports Authority (GTAA)**
Completed	**Phase 1: 2004, Phase 2: 2007**
Address	**Highway 427 to Terminal Access Road 1**
Transit	**Bloor-Danforth Line, Kipling Station, bus 192 Airport Rocket**
Access	**public**

SCHULICH SCHOOL OF BUSINESS

Located at the entrance to York University, the Schulich School of Business is an urban complex sited within a suburban campus. Offering undergraduate, graduate, postgraduate and executive education, the facility provides a refined home for business students and visiting executives. The immense breadth of this building's program is broken down into distinct volumes that create intimate outdoor spaces.

Three landscaped courtyards are framed by a series of limestone-clad classroom bars, punctuated by the vertical glazed volumes of the library and the executive tower. The remarkable curved corner glazing enhances the fluid exterior vocabulary developed in the limestone and ribbons of copper.

Cloistered promenades around the courtyards lead to meeting rooms and lecture halls, while the heart of the building is the three-storey atrium of the CIBC Marketplace, where a lounge and cafeteria allow students to gather informally. The quality of spaces and materials, both inside and out, creates an environment of uncommon sophistication on the York University campus.

Architect	**Hariri Pontarini Architects / Robbie/Young + Wright Architects Inc.**
Landscape Architect	**The MBTW Group & Janet Rosenberg + Associates**
Client	**York University**
Completed	**2003**
Address	**4700 Keele Street**
Transit	**Yonge-University-Spadina Line, Downsview Station, bus 106 York University**
Access	**university hours, www.yorku.ca**

CLAUDE WATSON SCHOOL FOR THE ARTS

The Claude Watson School for the Arts is a public school imbued with a spirit of imagination. Although built by the Toronto District School Board (TDSB) to provide specialized training in both the Fine Arts and the Performing Arts, it was constructed on the standard TDSB budget.

Sited next to high-rise residential developments, the building's bold exterior immediately announces that it is not a typical suburban school. Simple dark stucco, punctuated by strip windows, reveals a glazed ground floor that creates visual connections between the performance studios and the neighbourhood. An outdoor amphitheatre is nestled under the cantilevered library, whose brise-soleil nearly steals the show. Protecting books and students from the strong southern light, the aluminum honeycomb is accentuated by a lime-green window surround that causes it to glow, day or night.

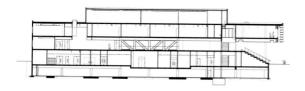

Architect **Kohn Shnier Architects**
Client **Toronto District School Board**
Completed **2007**
Address **130 Doris Avenue**
Subway **Yonge-University-Spadina Line, Sheppard-Yonge Station**
Access **private**

GEORGE AND KATHY DEMBROSKI CENTRE FOR HORTICULTURE, TORONTO BOTANICAL GARDEN

Strategically inserted into the site, the George and Kathy Dembroski Centre for Horticulture forges new relationships between earlier buildings and their natural setting. The sensitive addition maintains the integrity of the existing structures while allowing the gardens to be the central attraction.

This new armature building, located in Edward Gardens, frames a terrace and a well-planted courtyard, while establishing a new forecourt and entrance. Beneath its green roof, this glass pavilion dissolves into and reflects the landscape.

The interior of the pavilion basks in an ethereal soft light and affords ample views to the lush gardens beyond. From an atrium connecting the addition to the existing buildings, daylight cascades down the central stairs to the entrance of the Weston Family Library.

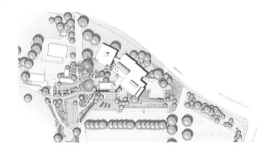

Architect	**Montgomery Sisam Architects**
Landscape Architect	**PMA Landscape Architects / Thomas Sparling Inc. / Martin Wade Landscape Architects Ltd. / Piet Oudolf**
Client	**Toronto Botanical Garden**
Completed	**2006**
Address	**777 Lawrence Avenue East**
Transit	**Yonge-University-Spadina Line, Eglinton Station, bus 54 Lawrence East**
Access	**public**

CNIB CENTRE

This unassumingly modern building houses a complex set of sensory experiences for Canadians who are blind or living with vision loss. The centre is widely acknowledged as an exemplar of Universal Design, focusing on spaces that can be perceived by all senses.

The capital cost of this training and teaching centre was financed through the sale of three-quarters of the CNIB's original ravine site, while maintaining the Bayview Avenue frontage for the new facility. As part of the design process, architectural plans were transcribed into tactile, thermoform drawings with Braille, as shown below, to convey the project to the visually impaired.

The interior is a world navigated by colour, texture, aromas and acoustic treatments. The straightforward circulation is bisected by a double-height café space, with an undulating wood ceiling and large windows opening onto the patio. Glazing is carefully considered to provide diffused natural light, while varying floor textures and contrasting colours enhance the user's perception of the space.

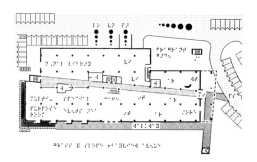

Architect	**Sweeny Sterling Finlayson &Co Architects Inc. / Shore Tilbe Irwin & Partners**
Landscape Architect	**Vertechs Design Inc.**
Client	**Canadian National Institute for the Blind**
Completed	**2004**
Address	**1929 Bayview Avenue**
Transit	**Yonge-University-Spadina Line, Davisville Station, bus 11 Bayview**
Access	**public, ground floor only**

BLOORVIEW KIDS REHAB

Bloorview Kids Rehab breaks the mould of a traditional hospital by creating a healing environment that reimagines the delivery of healthcare to children. Located on the edge of a ravine near Sunnybrook Park, the zinc-clad, L-shaped building takes full advantage of its natural setting. The distinctive sloping roof, designed in response to the zoning envelope, shelters outdoor healing spaces skylit by irregular cut-outs on the roof.

The interior is a tactile, playful environment designed for children and respectful of their needs. Children are encouraged to interact with the many artworks integrated throughout the building. Terrace spaces create outdoor playrooms, and for those not able to go outside, generous glazing and passageways provide a visual link to the natural world. The healing atmosphere is perhaps best evident in the ample communal spaces with child-scaled elements that encourage the long-term relationship between a family and the rehabilitation team.

Architect	**Montgomery Sisam Architects, Stantec Architecture**
Landscape Architect	**Vertechs Design Inc.**
Client	**Bloorview Kids Rehab**
Completed	**2006**
Address	**150 Kilgour Road**
Transit	**Yonge-University-Spadina Line, Davisville Station, bus 11 Bayview**
Access	**public**

THOMAS L. WELLS PUBLIC SCHOOL

The Thomas L. Wells Public School represents a commitment to healthy learning environments, community-led participation and design excellence, marking it as a leader and model for the future direction of educational design.

Designed as the first of a new generation of high-performance "green" schools to be built by the Toronto District School Board, the sensitively sited building translates the scale and materiality of its suburban surroundings in a contemporary manner. With the library at the school's heart, the classrooms are organized around a series of courtyards. Through the careful articulation of the exterior wall and placement of windows, the classrooms are generously daylit. In the library, the sloped ceiling and inclined columns lend the space a sense of dynamism, which is heightened by the treehouse-like resource room suspended within it.

Architect	**Baird Sampson Neuert Architects**
Landscape Architect	**Elias + Associates**
Client	**Toronto District School Board**
Completed	**2006**
Address	**69 Nightstar Road**
Transit	**Yonge-University-Spadina Line, Finch Station, bus 39 Finch East**
Access	**private**

SCARBOROUGH CHINESE BAPTIST CHURCH

The Scarborough Baptist Church is a hybrid building that dynamically houses a place of worship and serves many community functions.

Sited behind a woodlot in a suburban context, the metal-clad sculptural form of the sanctuary is an exuberant expression of worship. In contrast, the community wing is a rational, orthogonal form. The dual nature of the structure is revealed through Fellowship Hall, a central gathering place that links the sanctuary and the community hall. A simple material palette shapes enigmatic moments in the sanctuary, where the concealing and revealing of light heightens the transcendental quality of the space.

Architect	**Teeple Architects**
Landscape Architect	**duToit Allsopp Hillier**
Client	**Scarborough Chinese Baptist Church**
Completed	**2007**
Address	**3223 Kennedy Road**
Transit	**Bloor-Danforth Line, Kennedy Station, bus 43 Kennedy**
Access	**public**

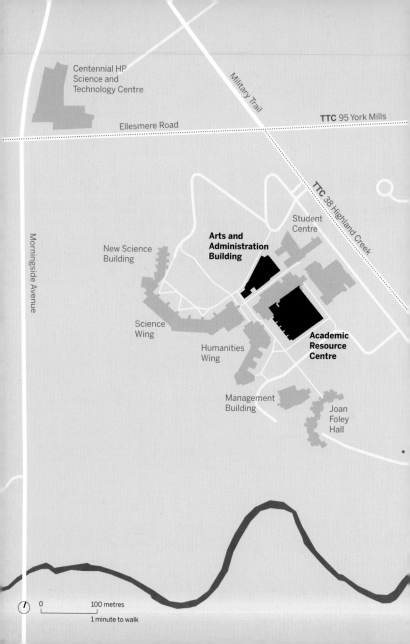

Centennial HP
Science and
Technology Centre

Military Trail

TTC 95 York Mills

Ellesmere Road

TTC 38 Highland Creek

Student
Centre

New Science
Building

**Arts and
Administration
Building**

Morningside Avenue

Science
Wing

Humanities
Wing

**Academic
Resource
Centre**

Management
Building

Joan
Foley
Hall

0   100 metres

1 minute to walk

UNIVERSITY OF TORONTO – SCARBOROUGH CAMPUS

The University of Toronto established Scarborough College on this ravine-hemmed site in 1964. The campus, designed by John Andrews, is an iconic cast-in-place concrete megastructure that bends along the edge of the Highland Creek Valley. Andrews' master plan proposed a phased development of a non-rectilinear campus. At a time of considerable university expansion in Canada, the college became an architectural landmark of the "New Brutalism" style that influenced the development of many iconic university buildings, such as Trent University in Peterborough, Ontario.

Though Andrews' master plan was never fully realized, a 2001 master plan by Baird Sampson Neuert Architects set the stage for the protection of the original campus and planned for its strategic growth. Through the Ontario SuperBuild program, the university received funding to construct facilities to meet the anticipated enrolment growth. This began the largest capital expansion program the campus had seen since its inception.

Other notable new buildings on campus include Joan Foley Hall by Baird Sampson Neuert Architects and Montgomery Sisam Architects, the Management Building by Kuwabara Payne McKenna Blumberg, the New Science Building by Moriyama and Teshima Architects and the Student Centre by Stantec Architecture. The university has also begun collaborative programs with Centennial College, which built the Centennial HP Science and Technology Centre designed by Kuwabara Payne McKenna Blumberg.

ARTS & ADMINISTRATION BUILDING

The Arts & Administration Building provides a ceremonial entry point to an ever-expanding campus. On the western, forested side, the soft hues of the limestone and buff brick extend the crescent form of the Science Wing designed by John Andrews. The slot and bay windows of the upper floors punctuate the taut brick exterior, while on the interior, a glazed pedestrian street recalls the wide, single-loaded public corridors of the original campus. At the western end of the building, a limestone and fritted-glass council chamber acts as a lantern for the campus at night.

Lush landscaping compresses the exterior space between the building and its undistinguished neighbour, forming an axial relationship with the Science Wing. Skirting the edge of this garden, a glass-covered exterior canopy creates a sheltered path between buildings.

Architect	**Montgomery Sisam Architects**
Landscape Architect	**Janet Rosenberg + Associates**
Client	**University of Toronto at Scarborough**
Completed	**2005**
Address	**1265 Military Trail**
Transit	**Yonge-University-Spadina Line, York Mills Subway Station, bus 95 York Mills or Scarborough RT, Scarborough Centre Station, bus 38 Highland Creek**
Access	**university hours, www.utoronto.ca**

UNIVERSITY OF TORONTO – SCARBOROUGH CAMPUS

ACADEMIC RESOURCE CENTRE

Located at the heart of the Scarborough campus, the Academic Resource Centre (ARC) is a rigorous contemporary response to the existing context. The ARC is a well-articulated industrial shed, whose massing and monolithic copper cladding references the rhythm of the lecture halls in the Humanities Wing designed by John Andrews.

This industrial shed houses a 500-seat lecture hall and a new central library, which are docked within the structural discipline of the building. These spaces are connected with black steel catwalks that are clipped within the structure. Concrete block is used in an alternating rough and smooth finish, recalling the texture of the board-formed concrete of the surrounding campus. Warm cherry wood is used throughout to designate intimate areas for studying or gathering within this industrial space.

Architect	**Brian MacKay-Lyons Architecture Urban Design**
Prime Consultant	**Rounthwaite, Dick & Hadley Architects**
Landscape Architect	**Hough Woodland Naylor Dance Leinster**
Client	**University of Toronto at Scarborough**
Completed	**2003**
Address	**1265 Military Trail**
Transit	**Yonge-University-Spadina Line, York Mills Subway Station, bus 95 York Mills or Scarborough RT, Scarborough Centre Station, bus 38 Highland Creek**
Access	**university hours, www.utoronto.ca**

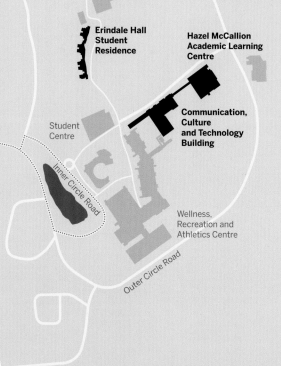

Erindale Hall Student Residence

Hazel McCallion Academic Learning Centre

Communication, Culture and Technology Building

Student Centre

Wellness, Recreation and Athletics Centre

Mississauga Raod

Inner Circle Road

Outer Circle Road

Mississauga Transit 1C Dundas

Dundas Street West

0   100 metres

1 minute to walk

UNIVERSITY OF TORONTO – MISSISSAUGA CAMPUS

Nestled in an affluent area of the City of Mississauga, the University of Toronto's Mississauga campus is situated on 25 acres of forested land along the Credit River. Founded as Erindale College in 1965, the core campus is a buff concrete megastructure defined by John Andrews' original master plan and elaborated by A.D. Margison and Associates with Raymond Moriyama.

Despite the rapid expansion of the campus, the university's policy of design excellence has urbanized this once suburban commuter campus. Recent building projects have focused on strengthening the public realm by creating courtyards and reinforcing axes as well as views to the forest landscape.

Other notable new buildings include the Wellness, Recreation and Athletics Centre, by Shore Tilbe Irwin & Partners, and the Erindale Student Centre, by Kohn Shnier Architects. Sited at the hinge point between the academic and residential portions of the campus, the Student Centre's success has become its biggest challenge, as student posters, banners and signage have obscured its minimalist aesthetic.

COMMUNICATION, CULTURE AND TECHNOLOGY BUILDING

On an axis between the existing campus and the new academic library, the Communication, Culture and Technology (CCT) building is an artificial landscape that contrasts with its natural setting.

Anchored by a linear circulation spine, an assembly of solid and transparent volumes frame exterior courtyards and establish new relationships with the natural environment. A curtain wall, tightly stretched across the façade, displays dazzling reflections of the surrounding forest, intermittently punctuated by projecting multicoloured glazing.

On the interior, mezzanines and stairs climb like jagged cliffs, connecting classrooms and labs. The dark metal-clad auditorium appears to crash into the building, depressing the topography of the floor around its entrance. The rugged material palette of concrete, blackened steel and glass introduces the industrial character of this firm's work to this pastoral campus.

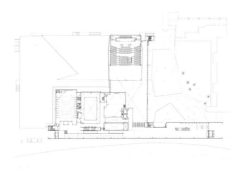

Architect	**Saucier + Perrotte Architectes**
Client	**University of Toronto**
Completed	**2004**
Address	**3359 Mississauga Road**
Transit	**Bloor-Danforth Line, Islington Station, transfer to Mississauga Transit bus 1C Dundas**
Access	**university hours, www.utoronto.ca**

UNIVERSITY OF TORONTO – MISSISSAUGA CAMPUS

HAZEL McCALLION ACADEMIC LEARNING CENTRE

The warm wood panelling on the exterior of the Hazel McCallion Academic Learning Centre signals the northern gateway of the campus. A Japanese puzzle box was the inspiration for the design concept, which is manifested in the shifting volumes of the exterior and the resulting interior voids. These shifts create a dynamic interior of interconnected spaces that form an array of places to study with varying degrees of privacy.

Designed with the requirement that all books be held in compact high-density shelving, the floor plate is kept free to allow for flexible, adaptable spaces infused with daylight. The library's circulation creates a sense of animation that is balanced by opportunities for quiet study in leather-lined private nooks overlooking the forest. A subtle volumetric shift of the building's exterior forms a rooftop garden that provides a vantage point for dramatic views of the CCT building.

Architect **Shore Tilbe Irwin & Partners**
Landscape Architect **The MBTW Group**
Client **University of Toronto**
Completed **2006**
Address **3359 Mississauga Road**
Transit **Bloor-Danforth Line, Islington Station, transfer to Mississauga Transit bus 1C Dundas**
Access **university hours, www.utoronto.ca**

ERINDALE HALL STUDENT RESIDENCE

This residence is sited alongside a meandering path and quietly nestles into a leafy corner of the campus. Modestly articulated and clad in red brick, Erindale Hall's subtle bending was a response to the natural topography of the site.

Framed by a series of tapered piers and an undulating wall, a colonnade invites pedestrians to seek shelter under it. The dazzling blue tile and fossil-rich limestone evoke a sense that the colonnade traces the path of a lost creek. At strategic moments, the stone panels give way to vast sections of glazing that offer snapshots of the forest through the building. Delightful and layered, this residence reveals a new reading with each visit.

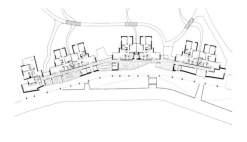

Architect	**Baird Sampson Neuert Architects**
Landscape Architect	**Janet Rosenberg + Associates**
Client	**University of Toronto**
Completed	**2003**
Address	**3359 Mississauga Road**
Transit	**Bloor-Danforth Line, Islington Station, transfer to Mississauga Transit bus 1C Dundas**
Access	**private, www.utoronto.ca**

TORONTO'S EVER CHANGING SKYLINES
SHAWN MICALLEF

Toronto has undergone an architectural renaissance in recent years that has seen construction cranes become as ubiquitous as the ravines – and raccoons – that define the city. If their skeletal silhouettes suddenly disappeared from the Toronto skyline, the void might be as noticeable as if the CN Tower had disappeared. The best way to comprehend how this tremendous growth has shaped the city is to compare aerial photographs of the downtown core from the 1980s with ones from today. The most striking difference in this comparison would be the vast number of parking lots and former industrial lands that have been filled in. In the 1980s photographs, the CN Tower and SkyDome seem orphaned from the rest of downtown, strangely shaped outposts on the western periphery. In the intervening years, they have been enveloped by the westward march of Toronto's skyline, making for a continuous cityscape.

Perhaps the clearest symbol of this reblooming was the destruction of the *Stump* of the Bay-Adelaide Centre. This rough concrete shell of a halted construction project had been left to stand as a modern ruin since 1991, emblematic of the recession that effectively ended the boom times of the 1980s. Located in the middle of the country's financial district, it was a warning to the leaders of industry peering down from their corner offices that economic booms end and skylines can stop growing.

What you can't see in those photographs is that as the vacant land was being filled in, solidifying the cityscape, Toronto's cultural scene was experiencing a similar growth. While construction filled in the physical spaces of the city, the *Cultural Renaissance* filled in Toronto's headspace, helping it understand what kind of a city it is. Urban construction in economically vibrant times doesn't just mean building physical things; the cultural landscape of a city can also grow, in between all the buildings. Like a warm and wet summer, the last fifteen years have been a flourishing time for culture in Toronto.

When I moved to Toronto in 2000, this cultural awareness was just beginning, but it wasn't something official, recognized and written about for others to come and see. It was nurtured in a feeling of collegial enthusiasm

Torontonians had for their city. As I discovered Toronto and witnessed how it was growing, I was pleased to find people who were as excited about their city as I was.

Construction and Cultural Waves

Historically, Toronto's waves of city building have been followed by waves of cultural growth. Toronto was often referred to as "Toronto the Good," a sometimes patronizing name that evoked a sense of colonial order but not a lot of excitement. Toronto grew, but it did so as a quiet provincial town in the shadow of Montreal, the city that was always seen as Canada's premier urban centre. Toronto's postwar boom began in the 1950s, and by mid-decade, the farmland of the outer boroughs was quickly being eaten up by subdivisions; a subway was being built up Yonge Street; and all over the city, modernist office and residential buildings were reaching skyward. Many newcomers arrived under the aegis of Canada's liberal postwar immigration policy. The Vietnam War also sent thousands of draft dodgers north from the United States, many of whom settled in Toronto. This influx began to loosen up provincial Toronto and, by the mid-1960s, the increasing bohemian, artsy and hippy forces reached a critical mass and turned Toronto into a "happening" place with a rich music and arts scene that, to the surprise of many, people travelled from other places to enjoy. At last, Toronto was interesting and, on the national stage, the city was growing out of Montreal's shadow. The modern buildings that came before and during this cultural ferment were a kind of concrete barometer of the city's fortunes.

At the same time, a civic activist movement was developing parallel with, and sometimes opposed to, all this modern building. Toronto matured – and learned – quickly. Whereas in the 1950s, the construction of the Gardiner Expressway was seen as heralding progress and opening up the city, it also eviscerated the west-end neighbourhood of Parkdale. By the late 1960s, citizens were ready to put an end to this practice, banding together to form the *Stop the Spadina Expressway* movement, which successfully blocked the construction of a neighbourhood-busting expressway. Though new buildings continued to go up, the municipal reform council, led by Mayor David Crombie in the 1970s, made it known that future city building in Toronto must proceed only with citizen participation.

It may not be fitting to apply the term "renaissance" to the immediate postwar era, as the city wasn't reawakening from a dark age, but rather coming of age, both physically and psychologically. Much-admired buildings such as New City Hall and the Toronto-Dominion Centre, as well as controversial structures like the Gardiner Expressway and the Don Valley Parkway, were signs of Toronto's metropolitan ascendance. Though much harder to quantify than physical growth, Toronto's arts and music scene began to burgeon in the streets and neighbourhoods, most notably in Yorkville. Into the 1970s, Toronto's reputation as a culturally rich place was described by Peter Ustinov's aphorism that the city was "New York run by the Swiss."

Though the city's cultural scene had by no means dried up at the end of the 1970s, the modern optimistic euphoria had. Toronto sustained its construction boom into the 1980s, but was no longer celebrated as a vanguard postwar city. Toronto was, in effect, coasting on a reputation built in earlier decades.

Our Contemporary Wave

Enter the recession of the 1990s and a mini dark age for Toronto, and we have a city ready for a real renaissance. Much as in the postwar building boom, residential towers were the first indicators of Toronto's rebirth. While the first wave of the 1950s had brought many new buildings and the occasional cluster of towers, it wasn't continuous. The contemporary wave is appropriating the spaces in between, filling in streetscapes and neighbourhoods. What this gives Toronto is an extremely heterogeneous typology. Toronto does not have a uniform look, but it is this urban mix that may, in fact, be the city's signature style.

Just as Toronto's current building renaissance was taking off, many of the Victorian and Edwardian structures were finding new uses. In the postwar period, these buildings were seen as past their prime and were demolished in the name of progress. By the 1990s, the municipal government had begun to embrace Jane Jacobs' notion that "new ideas need old buildings," and set about to rezone entire neighbourhoods, allowing former industrial buildings to be adaptively reused. This is most evident in the King / Spadina neighbourhood, which became the centre of Toronto's creative industry when rezoning allowed the transformation of onetime garment factories into productive loft spaces. For example, 401 Richmond, a former tinware factory, was converted into space for dozens of arts groups, magazines, galleries, and individual artists. Urbanspace Property Group, the building's owner since 1994, "curates" its tenant roster to allocate space to the creative side of Toronto – so much so that some often joke that if it burnt down, one-third of Toronto's culture would go with it.

On a larger scale, arts, environmental and civic-minded institutional development groups are also transforming unused industrial space in Toronto into hotbeds of design and culture. Artscape, a not-for-profit urban development organization that "revitalizes buildings, neighbourhoods, and cities through the arts" recently opened the Wychwood Barns, a former TTC streetcar garage north of downtown at St. Clair Avenue West and Christie Street. It has been transformed into a cultural hub through a well-designed retro-fit of the space for offices, a large meeting hall, artists' residences and even agricultural production.

Similarly, Evergreen, another non-profit group, works to make cities more livable and sustainable. It is converting the Don Valley Brickworks – a massive complex of buildings and sheds around a former quarry – into a place where cultural expression and environmental sustainability principles meet in equally impressive surroundings.

At the mouth of the Don Valley, another former abandoned industrial site, the Gooderham and Worts Distillery, has now been restored and retro-fitted with space for yet more artists, theatre companies, restaurants

and stores. All of these re-imagined places and spaces are reorganizing Torontonians' mental maps of the city and changing the places they work, think, play and live.

Torontopia

Although economically vibrant times often lead to culturally rich ones, the seeds of culture take time to germinate. It must be stressed that Toronto was never without culture, art and lots of activity – it's a big city and functions as such. But what began to happen in the early 2000s is very much like what happened in the 1960s: a cultural movement took over a large part of the city's consciousness.

The crest of this movement broke in 2003, when the results of provincial and municipal elections marked a shift in political values and brought into sharp relief what was going on in the city: a coalescence of the music, arts, literary and activist scene into what has been called "Torontopia."

Torontopia is most generally articulated as an unabashed love for this city. Torontonians, to a large degree, have shrugged off the inferiority complex that shackled this colonial city for so long and stifled its civic pride. While the old feeling of inferiority can still occasionally reveal itself, if this last boom has done anything, it has made citizens proud of being Torontonians.

Civic activists often join forces with Toronto's internationally successful indie bands to stage events that both celebrate and critique the direction of the city. Small arts collectives have orchestrated performances in previously under-utililized public spaces that send the message, "it's okay to have fun in Toronto" on a big scale. For example, the Scarborough Arts Council has staged installations at the Guild Inn atop the Scarborough Bluffs in the far east end and "New Mind Space" has thrown public events like pillow fights in Yonge-Dundas Square or "Light Sabre" battles in front of the Royal Ontario Museum. On the clandestine side, "Extermination

Music" stages music and art happenings in hidden abandoned places or in orphaned public spaces, like beneath the Bathurst Street Bridge along the lakeshore railway corridor.

Just as this wave was cresting I found myself in the company of a large community of like-minded Toronto lovers who were starting cultural projects – some small, some big – all over the city that were not just inspired by the Toronto of today, but motivated by the long tradition of positive civic activism that peaked in the 1960s and 1970s. I often wonder if today's movement could have happened without the earlier generation's work that demonstrated to us what is possible and, in a way, gave us a rough map to follow.

Surfing the Crest of the Cultural Wave

One such cultural project is [murmur], a mobile phone documentary project that I co-founded in 2003 in Kensington Market [murmur] finds people with a location-based story or anecdote to tell, records it, and puts up a green "ear" sign with a phone number in that spot. Passersby can call the number and hear these stories, narrated as through the person was speaking directly to them. [murmur] attempts to tell this city's stories on a small scale, building its nascent mythology, and counters the notion that nothing interesting happens here.

A few years earlier, a group called the Toronto Public Space Committee (TPSC) formed to advocate for improvements to the city's public realm. In addition to battling the encroachment of advertising in publicly owned space and lobbying city government on public space issues, the group's newsletter evolved into Spacing Magazine. Following the launch of the first issue in late 2003, Spacing Magazine became fully independent of the TPSC and slowly grew into what it is today: a tri-annual glossy print magazine with daily blogs on issues in Toronto and abroad. The magazine has evolved into the umbrella that coverers the "obstacles and joys" of living in Toronto and gives a platform for many small projects and initiatives across the city.

From the outside, these two projects may look as if they were carried out by a small, discrete group of people but the projects could never have started and gathered momentum without the collegial sense of Torontopia. I've always found it humbling how much people are willing share and help in Toronto, whether its younger folks and their energy or the older generation who were there in the 1960s and 1970s who suggest ways to actually get things done.

Both of these projects have found a home at the Centre For Social Innovation (CSI) at 215 Spadina Avenue. Located in another Urbanspace property, the CSI is a curated collection of individuals and organizations that each, in some way, contribute to a social or cultural good. The CSI functions as an incubator for non-profits that might not be able to afford office space of their own, like us, as we were operating from our bedrooms until we moved into our new home.

Toronto's Cultural Expression

Toronto's cultural expression is as heterogeneous as its architecture. On the green front, guerrilla gardeners have taken over derelict patches of land, planting long grasses, flowers and sometimes even vegetables. What starts out as political and environmental action ends up contributing to urban beautification. Festivals such as *Contact* transform exterior and interior spaces around the city – from billboards to bathroom walls – into one of the world's largest public galleries of contemporary photography. Perhaps the biggest showcase of Toronto's cultural ascendance is *Nuit Blanche*. This "all night contemporary art thing" sees over one million people take to the streets, wandering through neighbourhoods all over town looking at temporary, one-night-only indoor and outdoor art exhibits and installations. While the City of Toronto organizes the festival and has several "official" areas, various communities around the city produce their own events, giving *Nuit Blanche* an organic life of its own.

To truly witness the extent of Toronto's cultural explosion, one has only to walk west along Queen Street West from Spadina Avenue to Parkdale.

While the contemporary building boom is evident, the cultural boom is manifested in the many dozens of galleries that line the street. Nearly every block along these few kilometres has at least one cultural centre, be it a gallery or a venue like a bar or café; Queen Street is a machine that makes culture. The bricks-and-mortar cultural flagships are the Drake and Gladstone hotels, but the independent, ephemeral and guerrilla cultural scene is never far away.

The Next Wave

Toronto is never static. Even while a strip such as Queen Street West is operating at full power, new cultural areas are opening up. Neighbourhoods that once were thought of as peripheral to "where the action is" are now becoming hotbeds of culture and development. On the east side, the once relatively quiet stretch of Queen Street East through South Riverdale and into Leslieville has become the site of new galleries and, perhaps more important, the place where many artists and cultural workers can afford to live. Similarly in the Junction, an area that was for decades a down-and-out Toronto precinct is seeing an influx of artists who are, in their way, recharging the built urban form here.

Continued immigration not only adds to the city's celebrated multi-cultural character, but also intensifies the layers of development. Toronto's motto, "Diversity is our strength," describes the character of its built form as much as the nature of its population. The city moves fast, though. Even as I write this, there is a trickle of people moving out to what was once an unthinkable area for Toronto's creative class: the suburbs. As Toronto's neighbourhoods like the Junction and Leslieville grow and the inevitable development pressure arrive, residents will move farther afield into the former municipalities of Scarborough, Etobicoke and North York. While it will be a slow urbanization through intensification of the suburbs, in a few decades' time, another volume on Toronto's contemporary architecture will need to be published about the growing cultural strength of the suburbs.

What is now clear is that Toronto's urbanity has outpaced its built form. Even though Toronto has great culture and great buildings, its urban realm was designed for a provincial town. The city is awakening to the fact that great cities are judged by the quality of their public realm. City Hall has now established a public realm department tasked with a mandate to improve Toronto's pedestrian spaces. Civic activists have also begun to take on issues such as the quality of the street trees and cycling infrastructure.

Toronto continues to cultivate the rich public discourse that began in the postwar wave of development and has gone on into the contemporary wave. As the public realm wave crests, the discussion on quality of life issues is as likely to happen in a boardroom, a community meeting, an indie rock song, or in a gallery. In our new Toronto, the discussion on *how* the city is built will be as important as *what* is built. And the details will matter.

INDEX BY BUILDING TYPE

INDEX BY PROJECT

INDEX BY FIRM